THE OFFICIAL MAJOR LEAGUE BASEBALL PLAYBOOK

Edited by Chuck Tanner and Jim Enright

A Rutledge Book
Prentice-Hall, Inc.
Englewood Cliffs, New Jersey

Prentice-Hall International, Inc., London
Prentice-Hall of Australia, Pty. Ltd., North Sydney
Prentice-Hall of Canada, Ltd., Toronto
Prentice-Hall of India Private Ltd., New Delhi
Prentice-Hall of Japan, Inc., Tokyo

10   9   8   7   6   5   4   3   2   1

Library of Congress Cataloging in Publication Data
Tanner, Chuck.
   The official major league baseball playbook.
   1. Baseball. I. Enright, Jim, joint author.
II. Title.
GV867.T26   796.357   73-22020
ISBN 0-13-630954-2

Contents

1798518

A Comment on Baseball's Newest Rule

Originally, I accepted the new designated pinch hitter rule with reservations. I said I liked the game the way it was. Pitchers worked on their bunting, and the energetic ones tried to improve their hitting to help themselves as well as their club. I've always felt a pitcher's perfect execution of the bunt, whether he's sacrificing to advance the runner or trying to squeeze him across the plate, is one of baseball's best moments.

Now that the American League has approved the rule and used it for a year, I feel better about it. Any club with good depth can utilize the new rule to advantage. It helps a manager to rest his key players while still making good use of their hitting power and speed. On days when the White Sox desire to rest Dick Allen, Carlos May, Bill Melton, or Ron Santo, we can use them as DHs. As a DH, Allen is not only stronger through the season but also in a better position to help the club with his base stealing. Everybody talks so much about Dick's hitting skills that his speed is often overlooked.

A brand new future has been opened up for aging players: Tommy Davis with Baltimore, Orlando Cepeda with Boston, and Rico Carty with Texas, for example.

There is something very important in this new rule for managers and coaches from Little Leagues to the Babe Ruth Leagues to the American Legion statewide leagues. You don't have to bat your designated hitter ninth, in the pitcher's customary spot. You can use your DH where you figure he has his greatest value to the team. I'm not surprised that most designated hitters have been inserted in the heart of the batting order. Or you can bat a fast DH first or seventh. That way you can have speed leading off or a second leadoff man in the seventh slot.

From a public relations standpoint, it almost didn't matter that the DHs did relatively well last year. The new rule had already generated a couple million dollars worth of publicity for baseball, and especially for the American League. The pro and con discussions have been a big boost for the game. And in areas such as Chicago, where there are both National and American League teams, fans can see the game played with two different sets of rules and compare the differences firsthand.

Chuck Tanner
Manager, Chicago White Sox

Introduction

This book focuses on team rather than individual play because baseball really is a team game, even if it often seems not to be. Strikeouts, circus catches, and tape-measure homers are all individual feats, but pennant-winning is, as the victors invariably say, a team effort. Winners successfully defense the double steal and take advantage when the losers can't. The purpose of this playbook is to demonstrate how competent players become a winning team.

Not all major league teams do things the same way, so it is sometimes difficult for the editors of a major league playbook to decide which method is best. On occasion we have added to Chuck Tanner's prescriptions with those of other managers. Some plays, therefore, may be compilations of the ways of a number of clubs, rather than the method of any one club.

Finally, though this book concentrates on defensive play, because defense is more team play than offense, there is also a section of offense. Any playbook would be incomplete without one. Leaving the diagraming of plays to the defense, the section on offense deals with the strategy of the game as well as with the individual responsibilities of batter and baserunner. The reader will recognize, however, that neither the section on offense nor the one on defense is complete without the other. He may find himself learning offense while reading defense, and vice versa.

DEFENSE

Legend: In the diagrams in this section the following symbols are used.

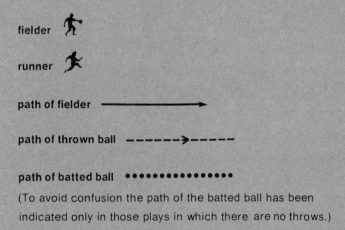

fielder

runner

path of fielder ⟶

path of thrown ball – – – – – – ⟶ – – – – –

path of batted ball ● ● ● ● ● ● ● ● ● ● ● ● ● ● ● ●

(To avoid confusion the path of the batted ball has been indicated only in those plays in which there are no throws.)

GROUND BALLS 1

Ground ball to the pitcher with no one on base

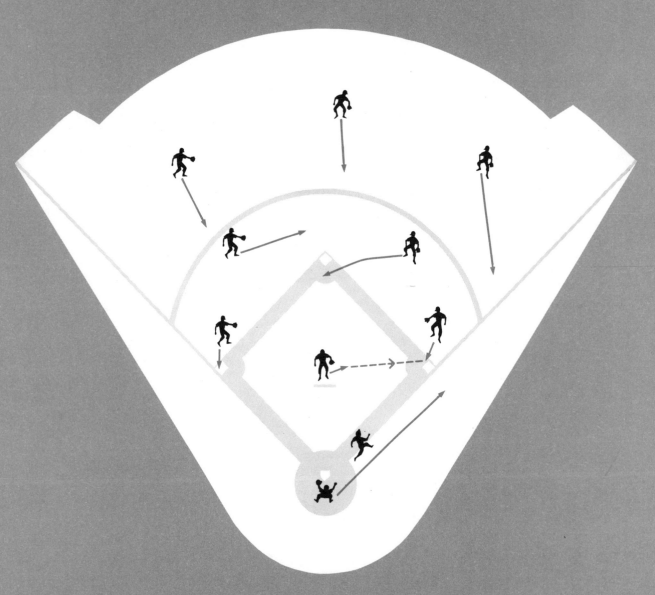

Basic objective: the play at first

The easiest play in baseball.

Pitcher: Field the ball, move toward first as you wait for the first baseman to reach the bag, and then throw to him.

First baseman: Cover first base and take the pitcher's throw.

Catcher: Follow the runner toward first and back up the base.

Right fielder: Move toward first in case of an overthrow.

Second baseman: Cover second base.

Shortstop: Back up second.

Third baseman: Cover third base.

Left and center fielders: Move toward the infield.

Note: With a runner on second base, the play is the same except that before throwing to first, the pitcher freezes the runner on second by looking at him, and the catcher covers home plate.

2

Topped ball or bunt near home plate with no one on base

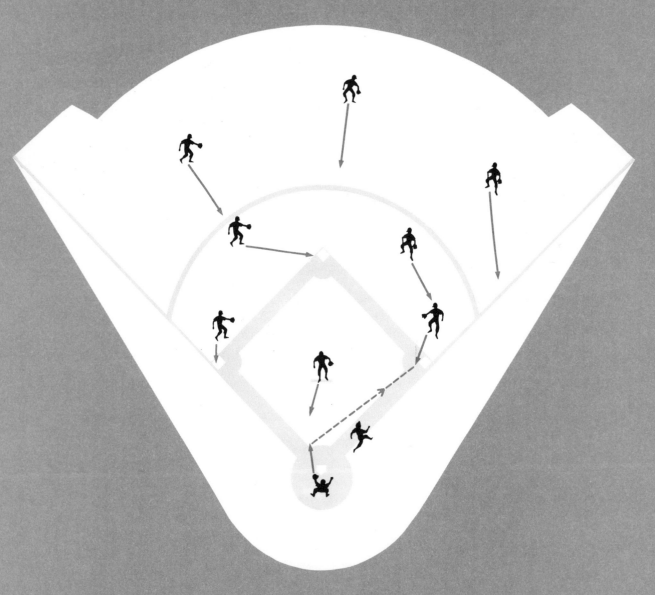

Basic objective: the play at first

If the ball is thrown correctly and it hits the runner, he will be called out for running out of the base line.

Catcher: Field the ball and throw to first, keeping the throw inside the base line to avoid hitting the runner.

Pitcher: Move toward the ball.

First baseman: Cover first base and take the catcher's throw.

Second baseman: Back up first base.

Right fielder: Move toward first base in case of an overthrow.

Shortstop: Cover second base.

Third baseman: Cover third base.

Left and center fielders: Move toward the infield.

3

Topped ball or bunt to right of the mound, past the pitcher, with no one on base

Basic objective: the play at first

This is one of the most difficult plays for the first baseman and pitcher to coordinate.

Pitcher: Break toward first base. If possible, field the ball and tag the base yourself. If the ball has rolled past you, move directly to the base, take the first baseman's throw, tag the inside of the bag, and move past it, away from the base line.

First baseman: Move after the ball, field it if the pitcher can't, and then toss the ball to the pitcher, underhand, shoulder-high, and slightly in front of him as he nears the base.

Second baseman: Back up the first baseman.

Catcher: Follow the runner toward first and back up the base.

Right fielder: Move toward first.

Shortstop: Cover second base.

Third baseman: Cover third base.

Left and center fielders: Move toward the infield.

4

Ground ball to the first baseman with no one on base (or with a man on third and the infield back)

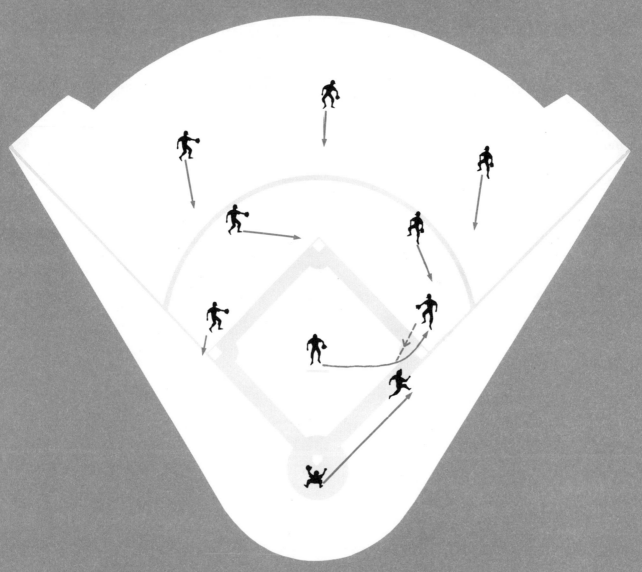

Basic objective: the play at first

The simplest and best way to make the play is without a throw, unless it is absolutely necessary.

First baseman: Field the ball, and if possible, tag the bag yourself. Tag the middle of the bag and move across the base line if the runner is far from the base. Tag the inside of the bag to avoid a collision if the runner is close to the base. If you cannot reach the base before the runner, toss the ball to the pitcher, underhand, shoulder-high, and slightly in front of him as he nears the base. If you field the ball far from the base and an overhand throw is required, throw directly to the base if there is time enough for the pitcher to plant himself there. Otherwise lead him toward the base with your overhand throw as you would with an underhand toss.

Second baseman: Back up the first baseman.

Right fielder: Move toward first.

Pitcher: As soon as you see the ball batted to the right side of the infield, move toward the first base line near first base. Before reaching the base line, turn toward first base so that you approach the bag parallel to the base line. If the first baseman has not made the play alone, take his toss, tag the inside of the bag, and move past it, away from the base line. If the first baseman is ready to throw overhand, you may have enough time to move to the base before taking the throw. In that case plant your right foot against the inside of the bag and take the throw.

Catcher: Follow the runner toward first and back up the base.

Shortstop: Cover second base.

Third baseman: Cover third base.

Left and center fielders: Move toward the infield.

Note: With a man on second base or men on second and third with the infield back, the play is the same except that the catcher covers home plate.

5

Ground ball to the second baseman with no one on base (or with a man on third and the infield back)

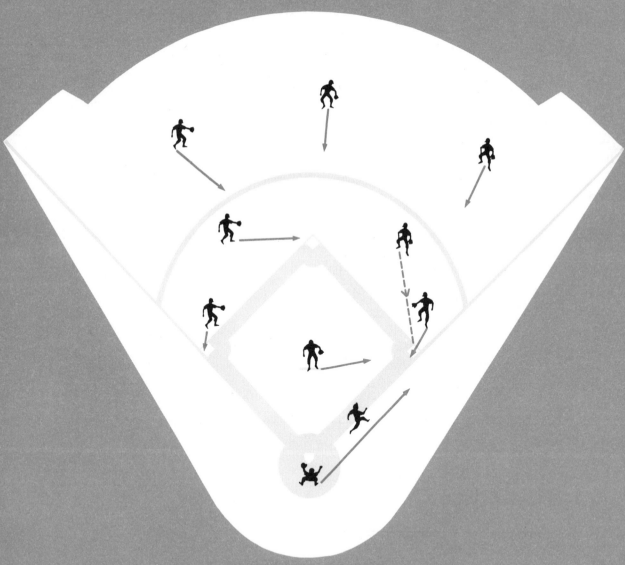

Basic objective: the play at first

The second baseman may have to wait for the first baseman or pitcher to cover first.

Second baseman: Field the ball and throw to first.

Right fielder: Back up the second baseman.

First baseman: Cover first base and take the second baseman's throw.

Pitcher: As soon as you see the ball batted to the right side of the infield, move toward the first base line near first base. If the first baseman is unable to cover the base, move to the inside of the bag and take the second baseman's throw.

Shortstop: Cover second base.

Catcher: Follow the runner toward first and back up the base.

Third baseman: Cover third base.

Left and center fielders: Move toward the infield.

Note: With a man on second base or men on second and third with the infield back, the play is the same except that the catcher covers home plate.

6

Ground ball to the shortstop with no one on base (or with a man on third and the infield back)

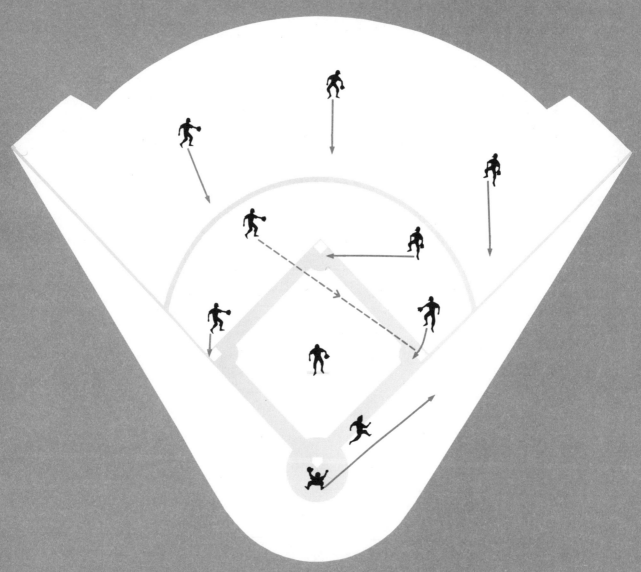

Basic objective: the play at first

The right fielder may be in a better position than the catcher to back up first.

Shortstop: Field the ball and throw to first.

Left fielder: Back up the shortstop.

First baseman: Cover first base and take the shortstop's throw.

Right fielder: Move toward first in case of an overthrow.

Catcher: Follow the runner toward first and back up the base.

Second Baseman: Cover second base.

Center fielder: Move toward second.

Third baseman: Cover third base.

Note: With a man on second base or men on second and third with the infield back, the play is the same except that before throwing to first, the shortstop freezes the runner on second by looking at him, and the catcher covers home plate.

7

Ground ball to the third baseman with no one on base (or with a man on third and the infield back)

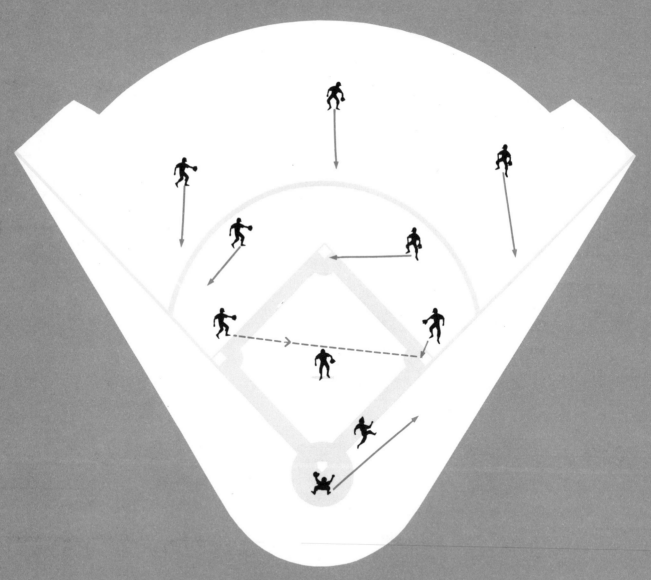

Basic objective: the play at first

The right fielder may be in a better position than the catcher to back up first.

Third baseman: Field the ball and throw to first.

Shortstop: Back up the third baseman.

Left fielder: Move toward third.

First baseman: Cover first base and take the third baseman's throw.

Right fielder: Move toward first in case of an overthrow.

Catcher: Follow the runner toward first and back up the base.

Second baseman: Cover second base.

Center fielder: Move toward second.

Note: With a man on second base or with men on second and third and the infield back, the play is the same except that before throwing to first, the third baseman freezes the runner on second by looking at him, and the catcher covers home plate.

8

Ground ball to the pitcher with a man on first and less than two outs

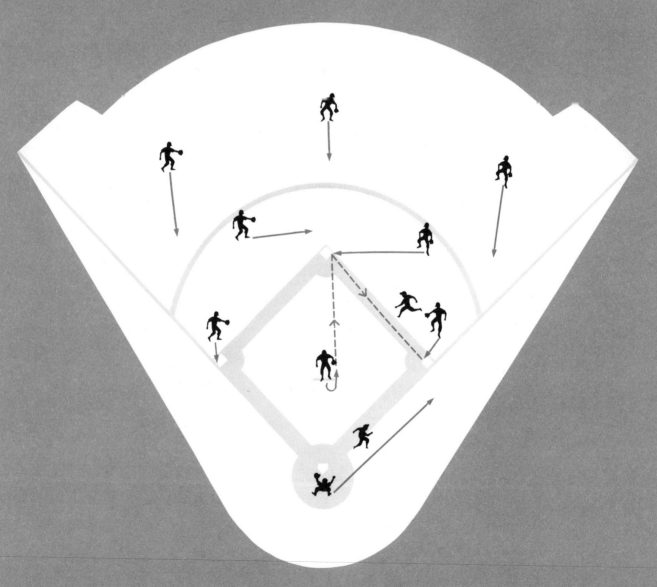

Basic objective: the double play

The pitcher should know where the man covering second wants the ball.

Pitcher: Field the ball, wait for the pivot man at second to near the base, and then throw there.

Shortstop and second baseman: Decide beforehand who will cover the base. The man who does cover takes the pitcher's throw and throws to first. The other fielder backs up the play.

Center fielder: Move toward second.

First baseman: Cover first base and take the throw from second.

Catcher: Follow the batter toward first and back up the base.

Right fielder: Move toward first.

Third baseman: Cover third base.

Left fielder: Move toward third.

Note: With men on first and second, the play is the same except that the catcher covers home plate.

9

Ground ball to the first baseman with a man on first and less than two outs

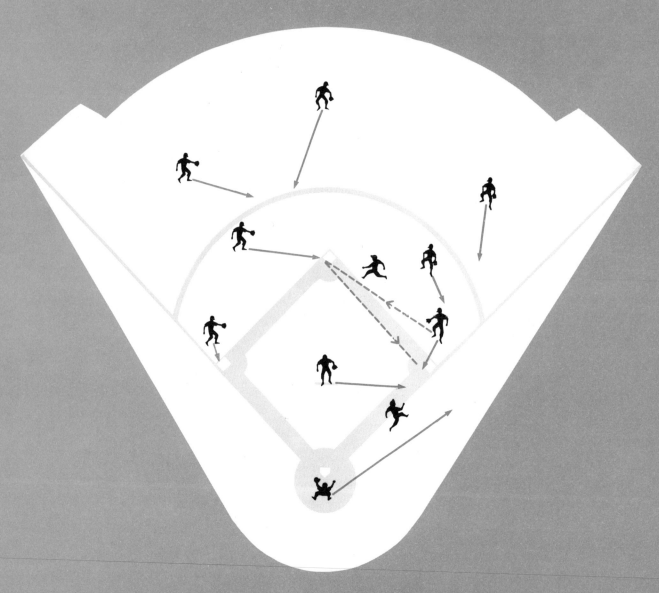

Basic objective: the double play

The first baseman should keep his throw to second on either side of the base line to avoid hitting the runner.

First baseman: Field the ball and throw to second. Then cover first base and take the shortstop's throw there.

Second baseman: Back up the first baseman and be prepared to cover first if he or the pitcher doesn't get there quickly.

Right fielder: Move toward first.

Shortstop: Cover second base, take the first baseman's throw, and throw to first.

Left and center fielders: Back up second.

Pitcher: As soon as you see the ball batted to the right side of the infield, move toward the first base line near first base. If the first baseman is unable to cover the base after throwing to second, move to the inside of the bag and take the shortstop's throw.

Catcher: Follow the runner toward first and back up the base.

Third baseman: Cover third base.

<u>Note</u>: With men on first and second, the play is the same except that the catcher covers home plate.

10

Ground ball to the second baseman with a man on first and less than two outs

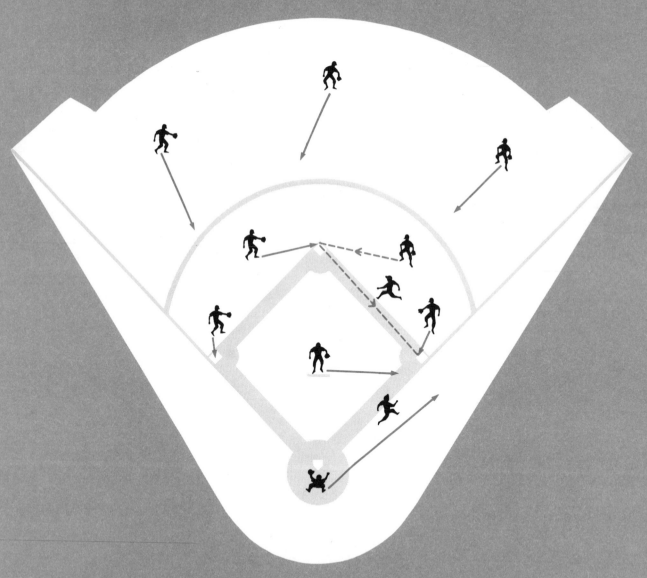

Basic objective: the double play

The second baseman should know where the shortstop wants the ball.

Second baseman: Field the ball and throw to second, keeping the throw on the outside of the base line to avoid hitting the runner.

Right fielder: Back up the second baseman.

Shortstop: Cover second base, take the second baseman's throw, and throw to first.

Left and center fielders: Back up second.

First baseman: Cover first base and take the shortstop's throw.

Pitcher: As soon as you see the ball batted to the right side of the infield, move toward the first base line near first base. If the first baseman is unable to cover the base, move to the inside of the bag and take the shortstop's throw.

Catcher: Follow the runner toward first and back up the base.

Third baseman: Cover third base.

Note: With men on first and second, the play is the same except that the catcher covers home plate.

11

Ground ball to the shortstop with a man on first and less than two outs

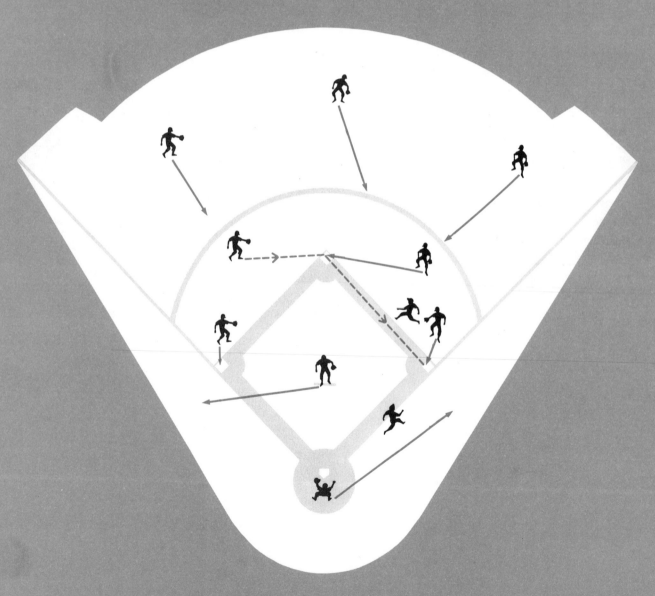

Basic objective: the double play

The shortstop should know where the second basemen wants the ball.

Shortstop: Field the ball and throw to second.

Left fielder: Back up the shortstop.

Second baseman: Cover second base, take the shortstop's throw, and throw to first.

Center and right fielders: Back up second base.

First baseman: Cover first base and take the second baseman's throw.

Catcher: Follow the runner toward first and back up the base.

Third baseman: Cover third base.

Pitcher: Back up third.

<u>Note</u>: With men on first and second, the play is the same except that the catcher covers home plate.

12

Ground ball to the third baseman with a man on first and less than two outs

---

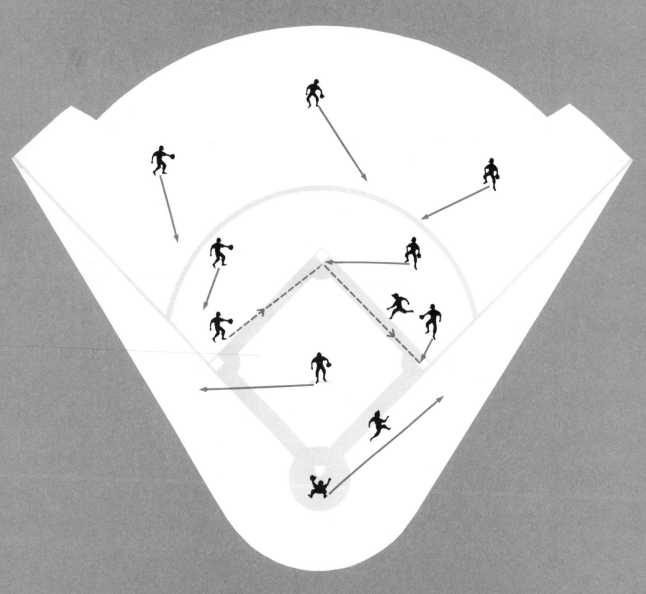

Basic objective: the double play

The third baseman should know where the second baseman wants the ball.

Third baseman: Field the ball and throw to second.

Shortstop: Back up the third baseman.

Left fielder: Move toward third.

Second baseman: Cover second base, take the third baseman's throw, and throw to first.

Center and right fielders: Back up second base.

First baseman: Cover first base and take the second baseman's throw.

Catcher: Follow the runner toward first and back up the base.

Pitcher: Back up third.

Note: With men on first and second, the play is the same if the third baseman fields the ball far from third base. If he fields the ball near the base, he can tag it and throw to first. In either case the catcher covers home plate.

13

Ground ball to the infield with the infield in, less than two outs, and a runner on third who breaks for the plate

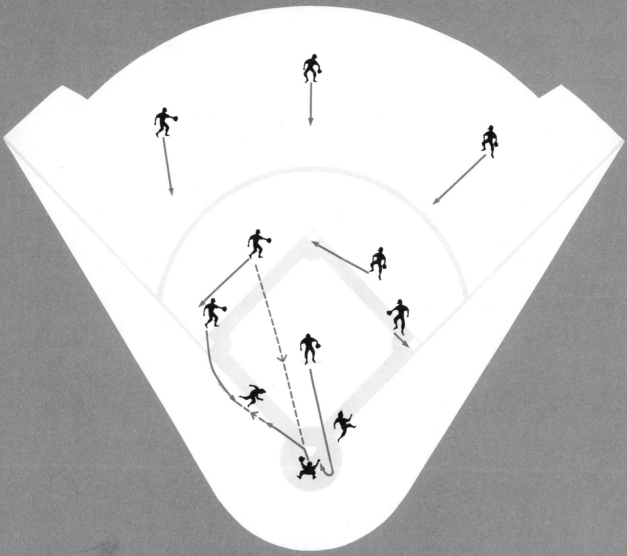

Basic objective: tagging the runner from third before the batter can reach second

The runner from third may simply try to barrel over the catcher, who should be waiting with the ball at home. More likely, the runner will head back for third when he sees he can't score. In this case the follow-in man, the third baseman, must be careful not to get too close to or overrun the runner.

Shortstop: Field the grounder and throw home. Then cover third base.

Catcher: Cover home plate and take the throw there. Move the runner back toward third and toss to the third baseman.

Pitcher: Move toward home plate and cover it as the catcher moves away, down the third base line.

Third baseman: As the runner from third breaks for the plate, follow about ten feet behind him. Take the catcher's throw and tag the runner.

Second baseman: Cover second base.

First baseman: Cover first base.

Outfielders: Move toward the infield.

<u>Note</u>: The diagram for this play shows a ball hit to the shortstop. For a ground ball hit elsewhere, the fielders' assignments remain the same except of course that a different man will field the ball and throw home.

With men on first and third and less than two outs, the manager must decide whether to have his infielders try to hold the runner at third or make the double play. Often the runner on third will break for the plate on a possible double play ball, intending to sacrifice himself in order to avoid a double play.

Unless the runner on third is vital and there is no one out (so a double play will not end the inning), a manager usually instructs his pitcher, shortstop, and second baseman to go to second on a ground ball, beginning what is likely to be a double play. This strategy allows the shortstop and second baseman to play deeper and reach more grounders than they could if they had to position themselves for a possible throw home. But the third and first basemen, whose throws to second to begin a double play are longer and more difficult than the pitcher's, the shortstop's, or the second baseman's, will be instructed to check the runner at third, to throw home if the runner breaks, and to throw to second only if the runner holds at third.

14

Ground ball to the pitcher with the bases loaded and less than two outs

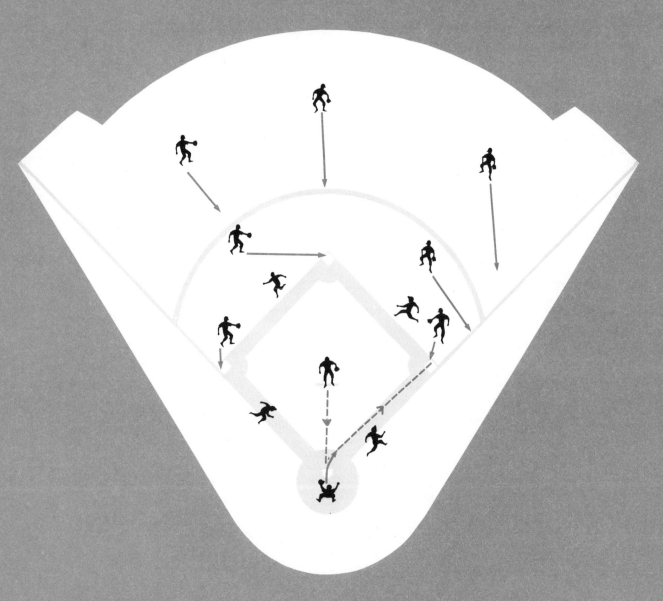

Basic objective: the home-to-first double play

Even if the batter beats the throw to first, no one will score.

Pitcher: Field the ball and throw home.

Catcher: Cover home plate, take the pitcher's throw with your right foot on the plate, move in front of the plate, and throw to first.

First baseman: Cover first base and take the catcher's throw.

Second baseman: Back up first.

Right fielder: Move toward first.

Shortstop: Cover second base.

Third baseman: Cover third base.

Left and center fielders: Move toward the infield.

Note: Infielders playing shallow in this situation will also throw to the plate after fielding a ground ball unless an inning-ending double play via second base is a certainty.

HITS

15

Single to left with no one on base (or with a man on third)

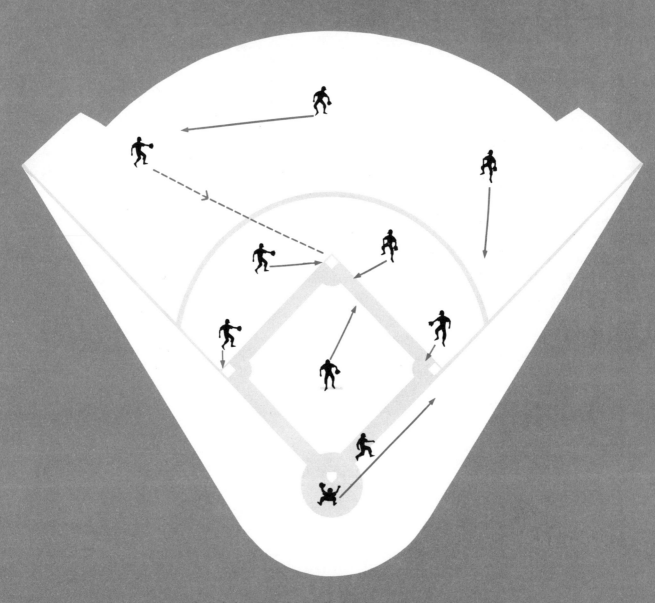

Basic objective: to hold the batter to a single

Three fielders cover or back up second.

Left fielder: Field the ball and throw to second.

Center fielder: Back up the left fielder.

Shortstop: Cover second base and take the throw.

Second baseman: Back up second, keeping the base on a line between you and the ball.

Pitcher: Move halfway between the mound and the second base position to protect against a wide throw.

First baseman: Cover first base.

Catcher: Follow the runner to first in case of an overthrow or rundown.

Right fielder: Move toward first in case of an overthrow or rundown.

Third baseman: Cover third base.

Note: If the shortstop is drawn toward third and the third baseman toward short in attempting to field the single, they should switch assignments.

16

Single to center with no one on base (or with a man on third)

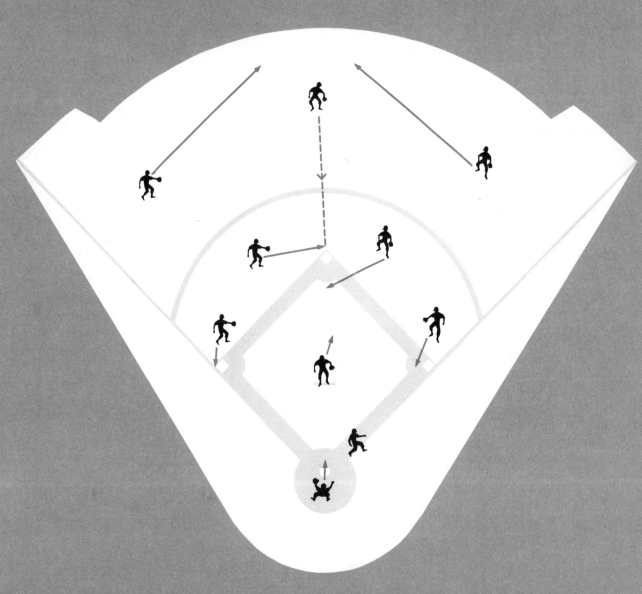

Basic objective: to hold the batter to a single

Three fielders cover or back up second.

Center fielder: Field the ball and throw to second.

Left and right fielders: Back up the center fielder.

Shortstop: Cover second base and take the throw.

Second baseman: Back up second, keeping the base on a line between you and the ball.

Pitcher: Move between the mound and second to protect against an overthrow.

First baseman: Cover first base.

Catcher: Move in front of the plate in case an overthrow gets past the pitcher.

Third baseman: Cover third base.

Note: If the second baseman finds himself closer to second than the shortstop, they should switch assignments. The shortstop and second baseman should decide beforehand, if possible, who will cover the base.

17

Single to right with no one on base (or with a man on third)

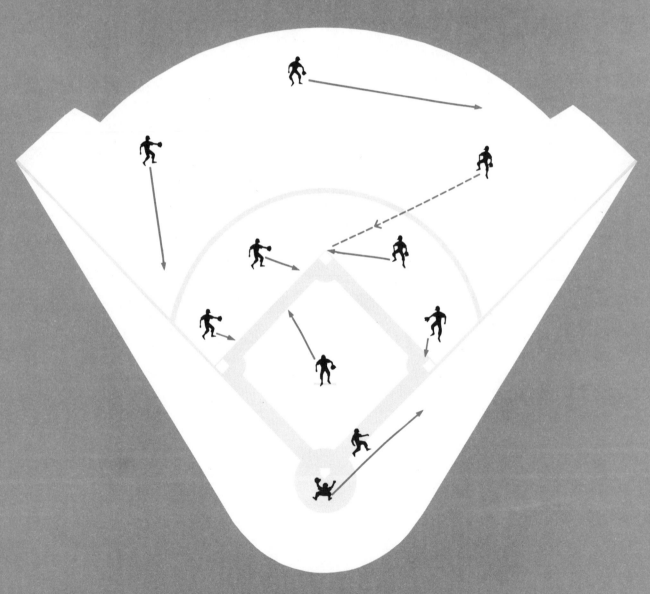

Basic objective: to hold the batter to a single

Three fielders cover or back up second.

Right fielder: Field the ball and throw to second.

Center fielder: Back up the right fielder.

Second baseman: Cover second base and take the throw.

Shortstop: Back up second, keeping the base on a line between you and the ball.

Pitcher: Move halfway between the mound and the shortstop position to protect against a wide throw.

First baseman: Cover first base.

Catcher: Follow the runner to first in case of pickoff by the right fielder, or a rundown.

Third baseman: Cover the third base area, being alert for an overthrow at second.

Left fielder: Move toward the infield.

Note: If the second baseman is drawn toward first and the first baseman toward second in attempting to field the single, they should switch assignments.

18

Long single, possible double to left center with no one on base, (with a man on second, with a man on third, or with men on second and third)

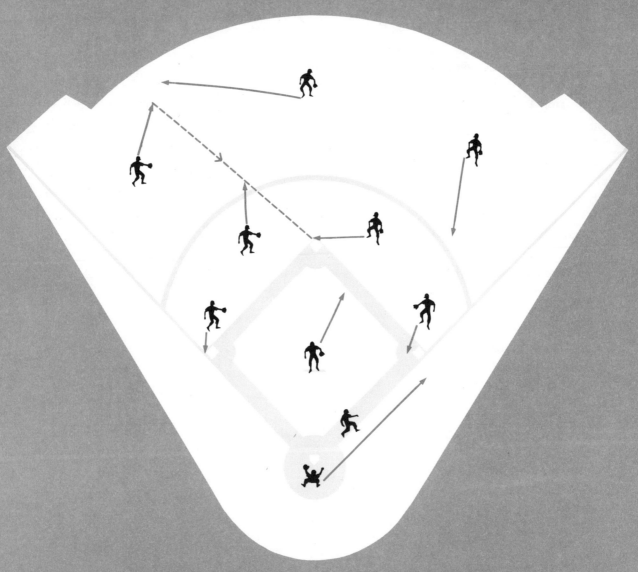

Basic objective: the play at second

A longer throw from the outfield may require a relay.

Left fielder: Field the ball and, using the shortstop as a guide, throw to second.

Center fielder: Back up the left fielder.

Shortstop: Move to the outfield grass, directly in line with the left fielder and second base. Following the second baseman's instructions, cut off the throw or let it through.

Second baseman: Cover second base, be prepared to take the throw, and instruct the shortstop whether or not to cut it off.

Pitcher: Back up second, keeping the base on a line between you and the ball. But be sure not to stand in the base line between first and second, where you may interfere with the runner.

First baseman: Cover first base.

Catcher: Follow the runner to first in case of a rundown.

Right fielder: Move toward first in case of an overthrow or rundown.

Third baseman: Cover third base.

Note: The diagram for this play shows a ball hit to left center. The fielders' assignments are the same for a possible double down the left field line. With a runner on second, the catcher should cover home.

19

Long single, possible double down the right field line with no one on base, (with a man on second, with a man on third, or with men on second and third)

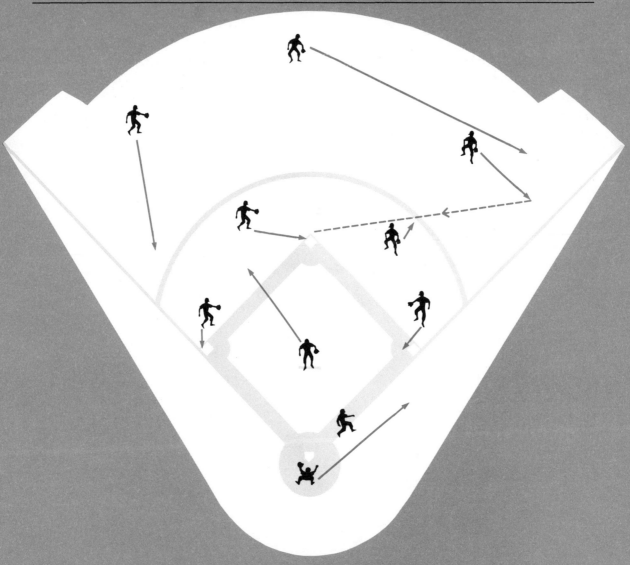

Basic objective: the play at second

A longer throw from the outfield may require a relay.

Right fielder: Field the ball and, using the second baseman as a guide, throw to second.

Center fielder: Back up the right fielder.

Second baseman: Move to the outfield grass, directly in line with the right fielder and second base. Following the shortstop's instructions, cut off the throw or let it through.

Shortstop: Cover second base, prepare to take the throw, and instruct the second baseman whether or not to cut it off.

Pitcher: Back up second, keeping the base on a line between you and the ball.

First baseman: Cover first base.

Catcher: Follow the runner to first in case of a pickoff or rundown.

Third baseman: Cover third base.

Left fielder: Move toward third in case of an overthrow or rundown.

Note: The diagram for this play shows a ball hit down the right field line. The fielders' assignments are the same for a possible double to right center. With a runner on second, the catcher should cover home.

20

Double, possible triple to left center with no one on base, (with a man on second, with a man on third, or with men on second and third)

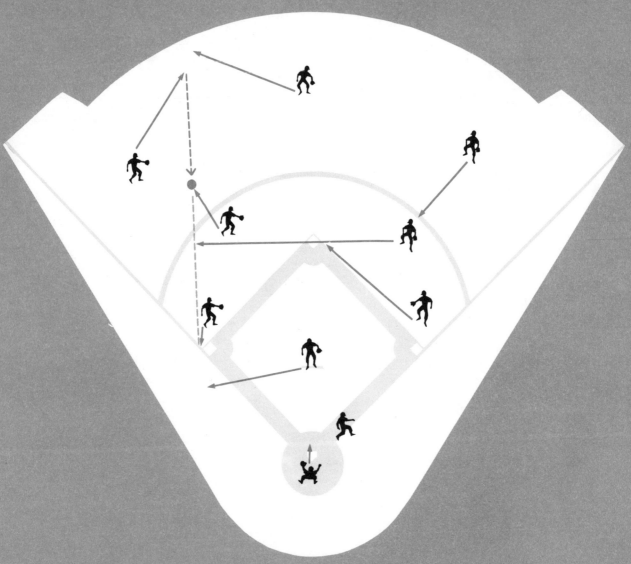

Basic objective: the play at third

Instead of covering second, the second baseman concedes the double and backs up the cut-off man.

Left fielder: Field the ball and, using the shortstop as a guide, throw to third.

Center fielder: Back up the left fielder.

Shortstop: Move to the outfield grass, directly in line with the left fielder and third base. Following the second baseman's instructions, cut off the throw or let it through.

Second baseman: Back up the shortstop about thirty feet behind him in line with third base. Instruct him whether or not to cut off the throw.

Third baseman: Cover third base and prepare to take the throw.

Pitcher: Back up third, keeping the base on a line between you and the ball.

First baseman: Trail the runner to second base for a possible pickoff throw from the cut-off man.

Right fielder: Move toward second in case of a pickoff overthrow or rundown.

Catcher: Cover home plate.

Note: The diagram for this play shows a ball hit to left center. The fielders' assignments are the same for a possible triple down the left field line.

21

Double, possible triple to right center with no one on base, (with a man on second, with a man on third, or with men on second and third)

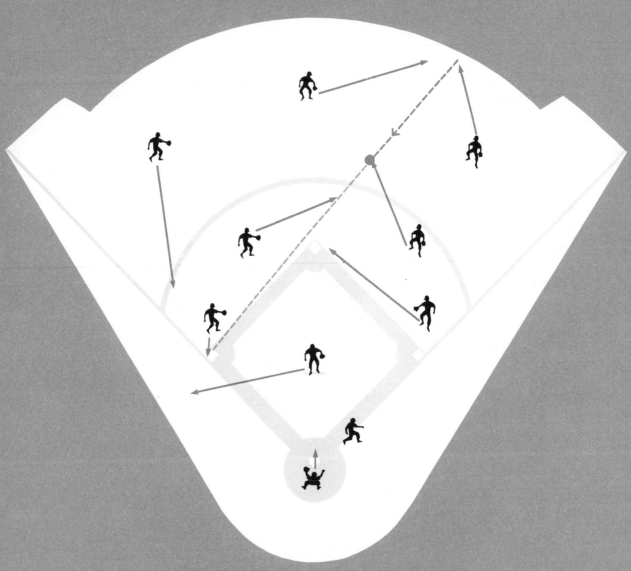

Basic objective: the play at third

50

Instead of covering second, the shortstop concedes the double and backs up the relay man.

Right fielder: Field the ball and throw to the second baseman.

Center fielder: Back up the right fielder.

Second baseman: Move to the outfield grass, directly in line with the right fielder and third base. Following the shortstop's instructions, relay the throw to third or just cut it off.

Shortstop: Back up the second baseman about thirty feet behind him in line with third base. Instruct him whether or not to relay the throw.

Third baseman: Cover third base and prepare to take the relay.

Pitcher: Back up third, keeping the base on a line between you and the ball.

Left fielder: Move toward third in case of a rundown.

First baseman: Trail the runner to second base for a possible pickoff throw from the relay man.

Catcher: Cover home plate.

22

Double, possible triple down the right field line with no one on base, (with a man on second, with a man on third, or with men on second and third)

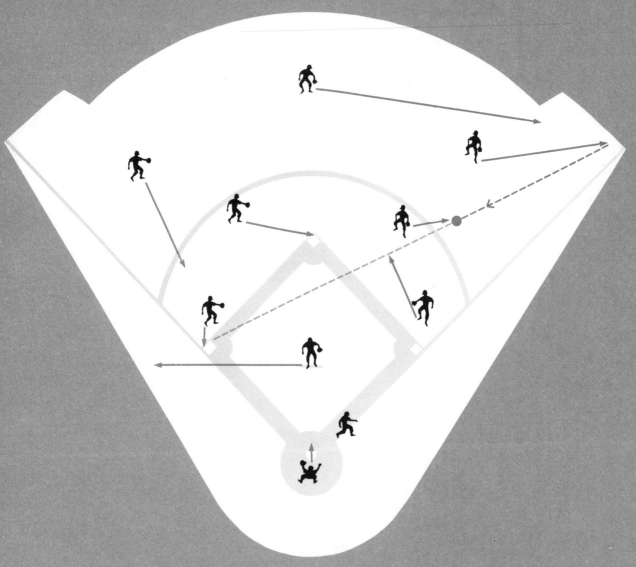

Basic objective: the play at third

The first baseman backs up the relay man.

Right fielder: Field the ball and throw to the second baseman.

Center fielder: Back up the right fielder.

Second baseman: Move to the outfield grass, directly in line with the right fielder and third base. Following the first baseman's instructions, relay the throw to third or just cut it off.

First baseman: Back up the second baseman about thirty feet behind him in line with third base. Instruct him whether or not to relay the throw.

Third baseman: Cover third base and prepare to take the relay.

Pitcher: Back up third, keeping the base on a line between you and the ball.

Left fielder: Move toward third in case of a rundown.

Shortstop: Cover second base for a possible pickoff throw from the relay man.

Catcher: Cover home plate.

23

Triple, possible inside-the-park homer to center

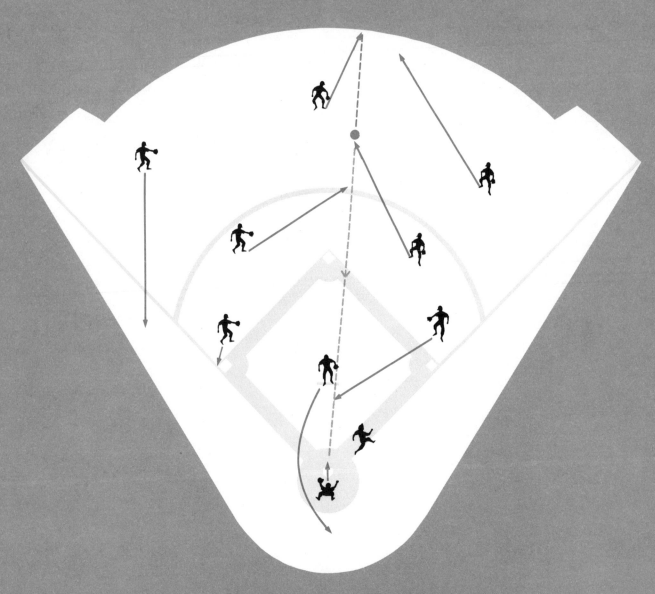

Basic objective: the play at the plate

On balls to the right field side of the center fielder, the second baseman becomes the relay man. On balls to the left field side, the shortstop becomes the relay man.

Center fielder: Field the ball and throw to the second baseman.

Right fielder: Back up the center fielder.

Second baseman: Move to the outfield grass, directly in line with the center fielder and home plate. Following the shortstop's instructions, relay the throw home or just cut it off.

Shortstop: Back up the second baseman about thirty feet behind him in line with home plate. Instruct him whether or not to relay the throw.

First baseman: Move to the infield grass, directly in line with the second baseman and home plate. Following the catcher's instructions, cut off the relay or let it through.

Catcher: Cover home plate, prepare to take the relay, and instruct the first baseman whether or not to cut it off.

Pitcher: Back up home, keeping the plate on a line between you and the ball.

Third baseman: Cover third base.

Left fielder: Back up third in case of a pickoff overthrow from the first baseman or the catcher.

Note: Though the inside-the-park homer is one of major league baseball's most infrequent plays, it is included here for teams whose playing fields do not have outfield fences.

24

Single to left with a man on first (or with men on first and third)

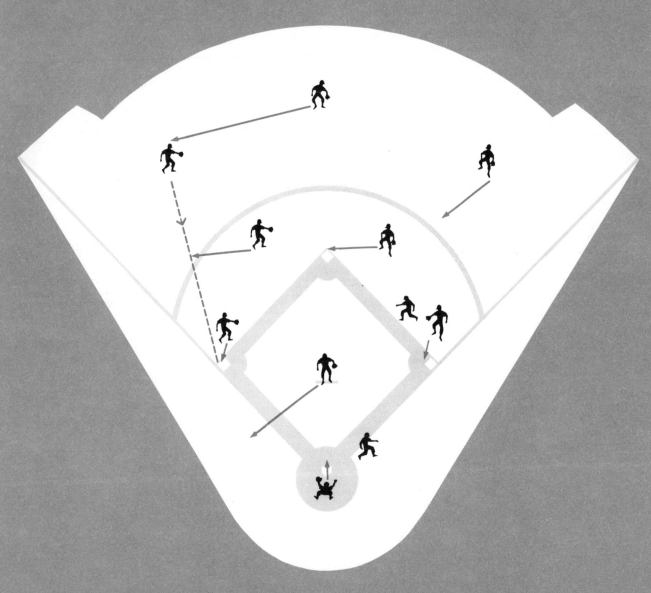

Basic objective: to hold the baserunner at second

This throw is often short enough not to require a cut-off.

Left fielder: Field the ball and, using the shortstop as a guide, throw to third.

Center fielder: Back up the left fielder.

Shortstop: Move to a position near or on the outfield grass, directly in line with the left fielder and third base. Following the third baseman's instructions, cut off the throw or let it through.

Third baseman: Cover third base, prepare to take the throw, and instruct the shortstop whether or not to cut it off.

Pitcher: Back up third, keeping the base on a line between you and the ball.

Catcher: Cover home plate.

Second baseman: Cover second base.

Right fielder: Back up second in case of a pickoff overthrow from the shortstop, or a rundown.

First baseman: Cover first base.

25

Single to center with a man on first (or with men on first and third)

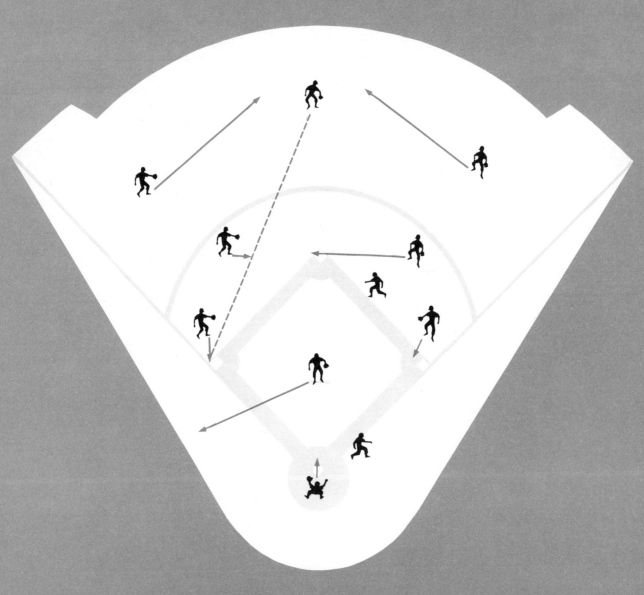

Basic objective: to hold the baserunner at second

The shortstop is in an excellent position for a quick pickoff throw to second if the runner rounds the base too far.

Center fielder: Field the ball and, using the shortstop as a guide, throw to third.

Left and right fielders: Back up the center fielder.

Shortstop: Move to a position on the infield dirt, directly in line with the center fielder and third base. Following the third baseman's instructions, cut off the throw or let it through.

Third baseman: Cover third base, prepare to take the throw, and instruct the shortstop whether or not to cut it off.

Pitcher: Back up third, keeping the base on a line between you and the ball.

Catcher: Cover home plate.

Second baseman: Cover second base.

First baseman: Cover first base.

26

Single to right with a man on first (or with men on first and third)

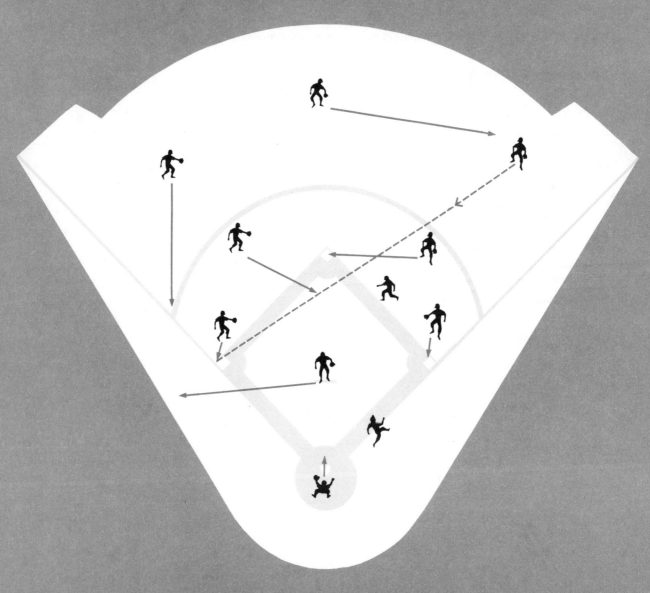

Basic objectives: the play at third and holding the batter to a single

The threat of the shortstop cutting off the right fielder's throw and snapping a quick throw to second base (or to first for a pickoff) should keep the batter close to first until the right fielder's throw goes through to third. By that time it will be too late for the batter to make second.

Right fielder: Field the ball and, using the shortstop as a guide, throw to third.

Center fielder: Back up the right fielder.

Shortstop: Move toward the infield grass, to a position directly in line with the right fielder and third base. Following the third baseman's instructions, cut off the throw or let it through.

Third baseman: Cover third base, prepare to take the throw, and instruct the shortstop whether or not to cut it off.

Pitcher: Back up third, keeping the base on a line between you and the ball.

Left fielder: Move toward third in case of an overthrow or rundown.

Catcher: Cover home plate.

Second baseman: Cover second base.

First baseman: Cover first base.

Notes: If the first baseman is drawn toward second and the second baseman toward first in attempting to field the single, they should switch assignments.

If the batter, in attempting to take an extra base on the throw, is an easy out at second, and there is also a chance to nip the lead runner at third, be sure to get the sure out—the runner going to second.

27

Long single, possible double down the left field line with a man on first, (with men on first and second, with men on first and third, or with the bases loaded)

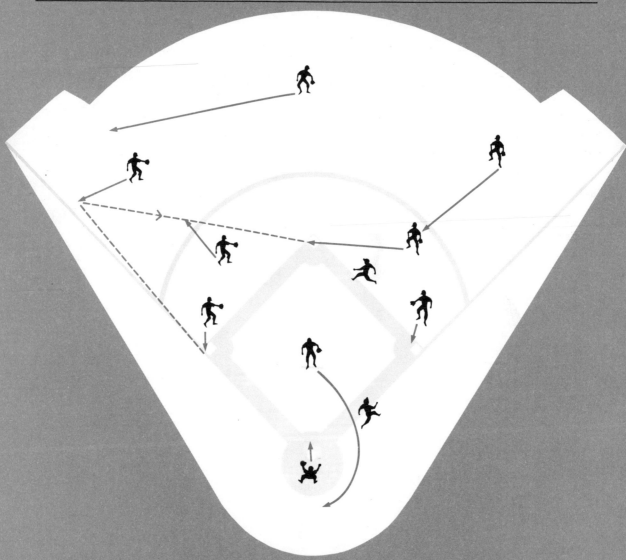

Basic objective: the play at second

If the batter has a chance of reaching second, the runner on first will usually make third easily.

Left fielder: Field the ball and, using the shortstop as a guide, throw to second.

Center fielder: Back up the left fielder.

Shortstop: Move to the outfield grass, directly in line with the left fielder and second base. Following the second baseman's instructions, cut off the throw or let it through.

Second baseman: Cover second base, prepare to take the throw, and instruct the shortstop whether or not to cut it off.

Right fielder: Move toward the infield in case of an overthrow at second.

First baseman: Cover first base.

Third baseman: Cover third base.

Catcher: Cover home plate.

Pitcher: Back up home.

Note: The diagram for this play shows a ball hit down the left field line. The fielders' assignments are the same for a possible double to left center.

28

Long single, possible double to right center with a man on first, (with men on first and second, with men on first and third, or with the bases loaded)

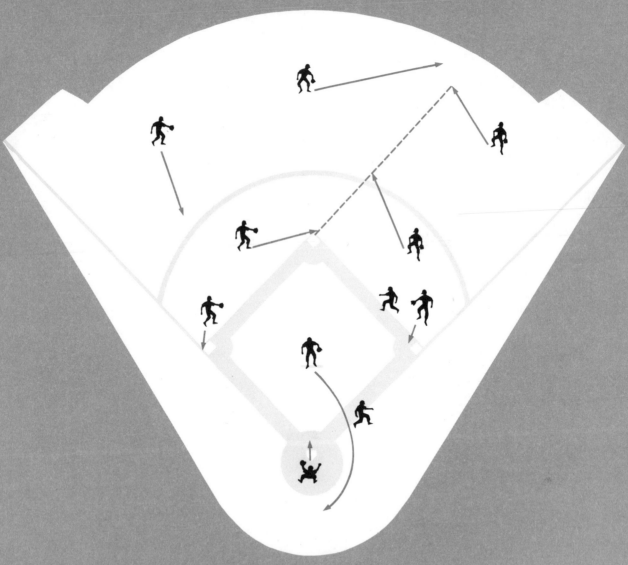

Basic objective: the play at second

If the batter has a chance of reaching second, the runner on first will usually make third easily.

Right fielder: Field the ball and, using the second baseman as a guide, throw to second.

Center fielder: Back up the right fielder.

Second baseman: Move to the outfield grass, directly in line with the right fielder and second base. Following the shortstop's instructions, cut off the throw or let it through.

Shortstop: Cover second base, prepare to take the throw, and instruct the second baseman whether or not to cut it off.

Left fielder: Move toward the infield in case of an overthrow at second.

First baseman: Cover first base.

Third baseman: Cover third base.

Catcher: Cover home plate.

Pitcher: Back up home.

Note: The diagram for this play shows a ball hit to right center. The fielders' assignments are the same for a possible double down the right field line.

29

Double, possible triple to left center with a man on first, (with men on first and second, with men on first and third, or with the bases loaded)

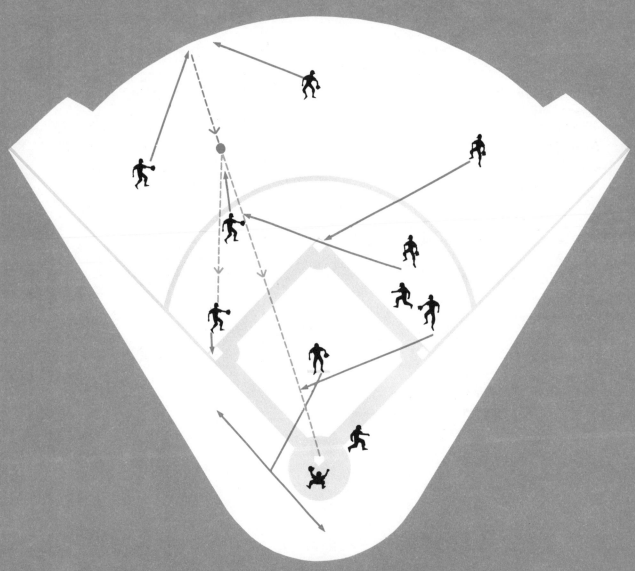

Basic objective: the play at the plate or the play at third

66

There is a relay man and a cut-off man.

Left fielder: Field the ball and throw to the shortstop.

Center fielder: Back up the left fielder.

Shortstop: Move to the outfield grass, directly in line with the left fielder and home plate. Following the second baseman's instructions, relay the throw either to the plate, using the first baseman as a guide, or to third. Or, just cut off the throw.

Second baseman: Back up the shortstop about thirty feet behind him in line with the plate. Instruct him where to relay the throw (to the plate or to third). Or, tell him just to cut it off.

First baseman: Move to the infield grass, directly in line with the shortstop and home plate. Following the catcher's instructions (if the relay comes toward the plate), cut off the relay or let it through.

Catcher: Cover home plate. If the relay comes toward the plate, prepare to take it, and instruct the first baseman whether or not to cut it off.

Pitcher: Move to a position outside the third base line, close to home plate. Back up the base to which the throw goes—either home or third.

Third baseman: Cover third base and take the relay if it comes there.

Right fielder: Cover second base.

30

Double, possible triple down the left field line with a man on first, (with men on first and second, with men on first and third, or with the bases loaded)

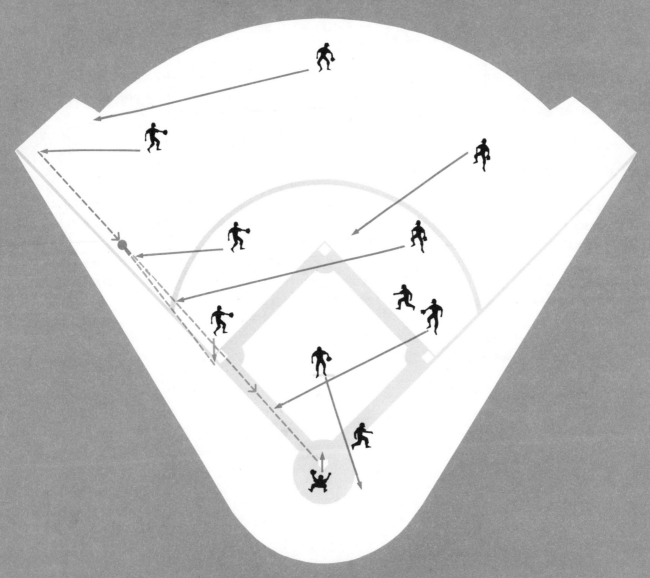

Basic objective: the play at the plate or the play at third.

There is a relay man and a cut-off man.

Left fielder: Field the ball and throw to the shortstop.

Center fielder: Back up the left fielder.

Shortstop: Move to the outfield grass, directly in line with the left fielder and home plate. Following the second baseman's instructions, relay the throw either to the plate, using the first baseman as a guide, or to third. Or, if there is no play at either base, just cut off the throw.

Second baseman: Back up the shortstop about thirty feet behind him in line with the plate. Instruct him where to relay the throw (to the plate or to third). Or, if there is no play at either base, tell him just to cut off the throw.

First baseman: Move to the third base line between home and third, directly in line with the shortstop and home plate. Following the catcher's instructions (if the relay comes toward the plate), cut off the relay or let it through.

Catcher: Cover home plate. If the relay comes toward the plate, prepare to take it, and instruct the first baseman whether or not to cut it off.

Pitcher: Back up home, keeping the plate on a line between you and the ball.

Third baseman: Cover third base and take the relay if it comes there.

Right fielder: Cover second base.

31

Double, possible triple to right center with a man on first, (with men on first and second, with men on first and third, or with the bases loaded)

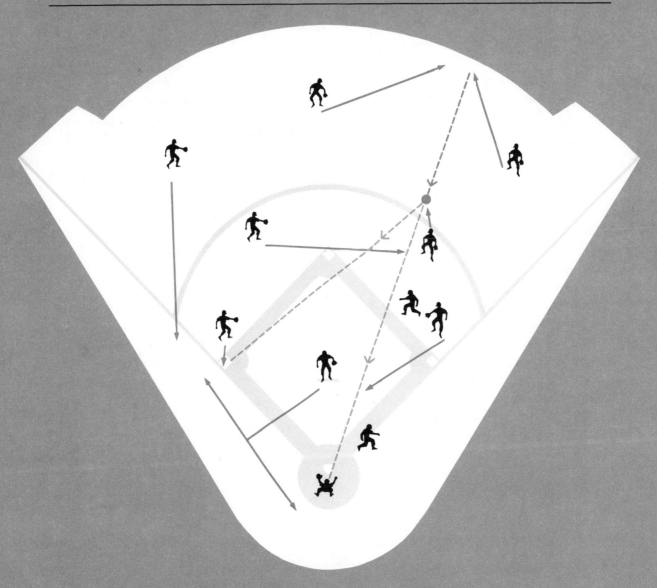

Basic objective: the play at the plate or the play at third

There is a relay man and a cut-off man.

Right fielder: Field the ball and throw to the second baseman.

Center fielder: Back up the right fielder.

Second baseman: Move to the outfield grass, directly in line with the right fielder and home plate. Following the shortstop's instructions, relay the throw either to the plate, using the first baseman as a guide, or to third. Or, if there is no play at either base, just cut off the throw.

Shortstop: Back up the second baseman about thirty feet behind him in line with the plate. Instruct him where to relay the throw (to the plate or to third). Or, if there is no play at either base, tell him just to cut off the throw. Then cover second base.

First baseman: Move to the infield grass, directly in line with the second baseman and home plate. Following the catcher's instructions (if the relay comes toward the plate), cut off the relay or let it through.

Catcher: Cover home plate. If the relay comes toward the plate, prepare to take it, and instruct the first baseman whether or not to cut it off.

Pitcher: Move to a position outside the third base line, between third and home. Back up the base to which the throw goes—either home or third.

Third baseman: Cover third base and take the relay if it comes there.

Left fielder: Back up third in line with the first baseman in case he cuts off a relay to the plate and throws to third.

32

Double, possible triple down the right field line with a man on first, (with men on first and second, with men on first and third, or with the bases loaded)

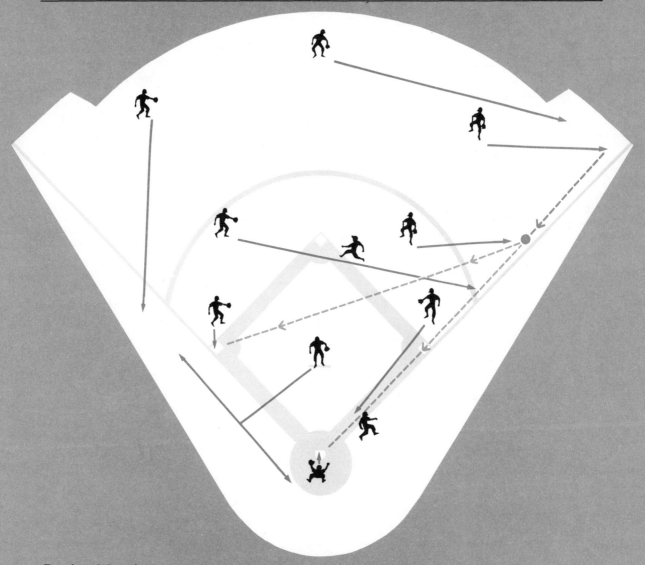

Basic objective: the play at the plate or the play at third

There is a relay man and a cut-off man.

Right fielder: Field the ball and throw to the second baseman.

Center fielder: Back up the right fielder.

Second baseman: Move to the outfield grass, directly in line with the right fielder and home plate. Following the shortstop's instructions, relay the throw either to the plate, using the first baseman as a guide, or to third. Or, if there is no play at either base, just cut off the throw.

Shortstop: Back up the second baseman about thirty feet behind him in line with the plate. Instruct him where to relay the throw (to the plate or to third). Or, if there is no play at either base, tell him just to cut off the throw.

First baseman: Move down the first base line toward home, to a position in line with the second baseman and home plate. Following the catcher's instructions (if the relay comes toward the plate), cut off the relay or let it through.

Catcher: Cover home plate. If the relay comes toward the plate, prepare to take it, and instruct the first baseman whether or not to cut it off.

Pitcher: Move to a position outside the third base line, between third and home. Back up the base to which the throw goes—either home or third.

Third baseman: Cover third base and take the relay if it comes there.

Left fielder: Back up third in line with first baseman in case he cuts off a relay to the plate and throws to third.

Note: On this play second base is left uncovered.

33

Single to left with a man on second (or with men on second and third)

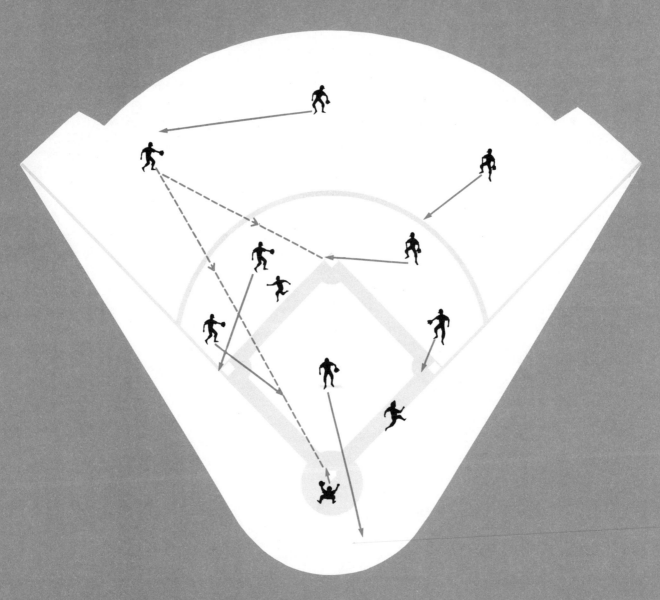

Basic objectives: the play at the plate and holding the batter to a single

Never let the tying run get into scoring position at second base by throwing to the plate when the runner is likely to score.

Left fielder: Field the ball and throw either to the plate, using the third baseman as a guide, or to second.

Center fielder: Back up the left fielder.

Third baseman: Move to the infield grass, directly in line with the left fielder and home plate. Following the catcher's instructions (if the throw comes toward the plate), cut off the throw or let it through.

Catcher: Cover home plate. If the throw comes toward the plate, prepare to take it, and instruct the third baseman whether or not to cut it off.

Pitcher: Back up home, keeping the plate on a line between you and the ball.

Second baseman: Cover second base and take the throw if it comes there.

Right fielder: Move toward infield in case of overthrow at second.

Shortstop: Cover third base.

First baseman: Cover first base.

34

Single to center with a man on second (or with men on second and third)

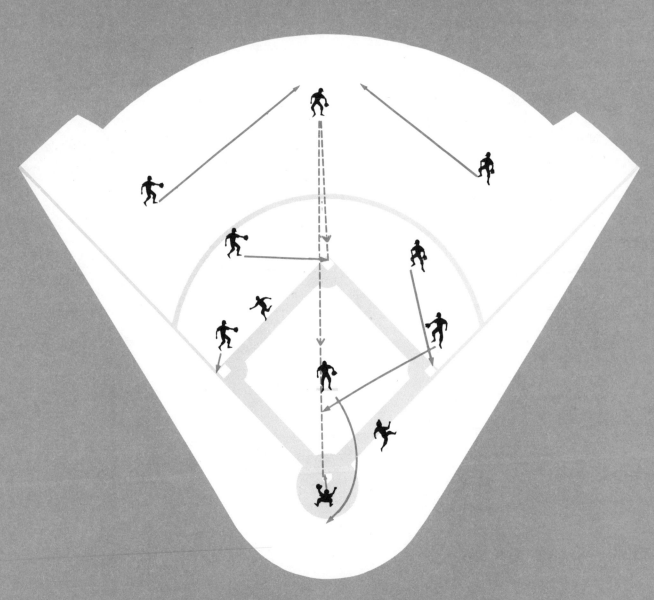

Basic objectives: the play at the plate and holding the batter to a single

Never let the tying run get into scoring position at second base by throwing to the plate when the runner is likely to score.

Center fielder: Field the ball and throw either to the plate, using the first baseman as a guide, or to second.

Left and right fielders: Back up the center fielder.

First baseman: Move to the infield grass, directly in line with the center fielder and home plate. Following the catcher's instructions (if the throw comes toward the plate), cut off the throw or let it through.

Catcher: Cover home plate. If the throw comes toward the plate, prepare to take it, and instruct the first baseman whether or not to cut it off.

Pitcher: Back up home, keeping the plate on a line between you and the ball.

Shortstop: Cover second base and take the throw if it comes there.

Third baseman: Cover third base.

Second baseman: Cover first base.

35

Single to right field with a man on second (or with men on second and third)

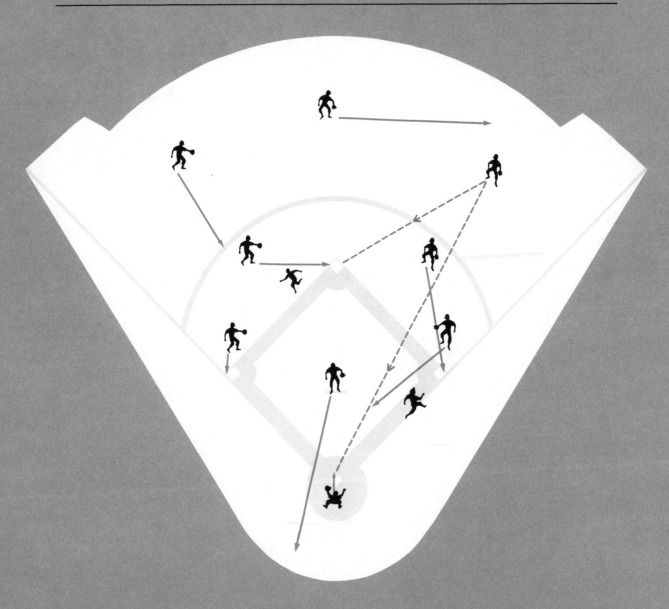

Basic objectives: the play at the plate and holding the batter to a single

Never let the tying run get into scoring position at second base by throwing to the plate when the runner is likely to score.

Right fielder: Field the ball and throw either to the plate, using the first baseman as a guide, or to second.

Center fielder: Back up the right fielder.

First baseman: Move to the infield grass, directly in line with the right fielder and home plate. Following the catcher's instructions (if the throw comes toward home plate), cut off the throw or let it through.

Catcher: Cover home plate. If the throw comes toward the plate, prepare to take it, and instruct the first baseman whether or not to cut it off.

Pitcher: Back up home, keeping the plate on a line between you and the ball.

Shortstop: Cover second base and take the throw if it comes there.

Third baseman: Cover third base.

Left fielder: Move toward the infield in case of an overthrow or rundown.

Second baseman: Cover first base.

36

Single to left with men on first and second (or with the bases loaded)

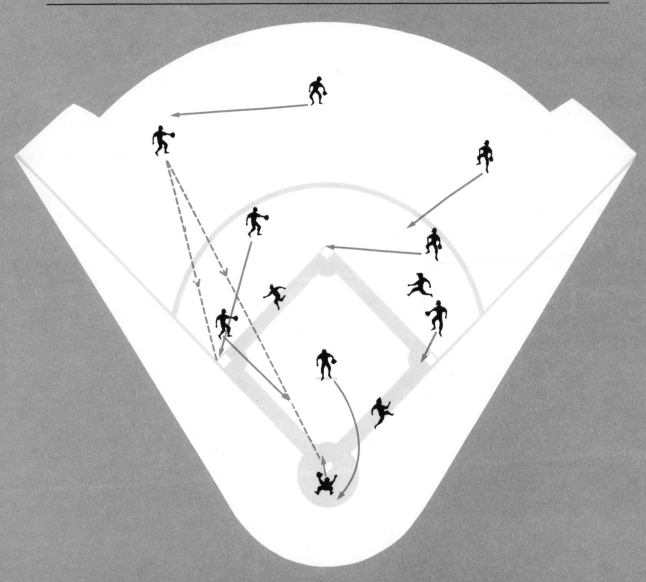

Basic objectives: the play at the plate and holding the baserunner from first to one base

With less than two outs, never let the tying or winning run go to third.

Left fielder: Field the ball and throw either to the plate, using the third baseman as a guide, or to third.

Center fielder: Back up the left fielder.

Third baseman: Move to the infield grass, directly in line with the left fielder and home plate. Following the catcher's instructions (if the throw comes toward home), cut off the throw or let it through.

Catcher: Cover home plate. If the throw comes toward home, prepare to take it, and instruct the third baseman whether or not to cut it off.

Pitcher: Back up home, keeping the plate on a line between you and the ball.

Shortstop: Cover third base and take the throw if it comes there.

Second baseman: Cover second base.

Right fielder: Back up second in case of a rundown.

First baseman: Cover first base.

Note: The positions for this play combine those for two previous plays: 24 (single to left with a man on first), and 33 (single to left with a man on second).

37

Single to center with men on first and second (or with the bases loaded)

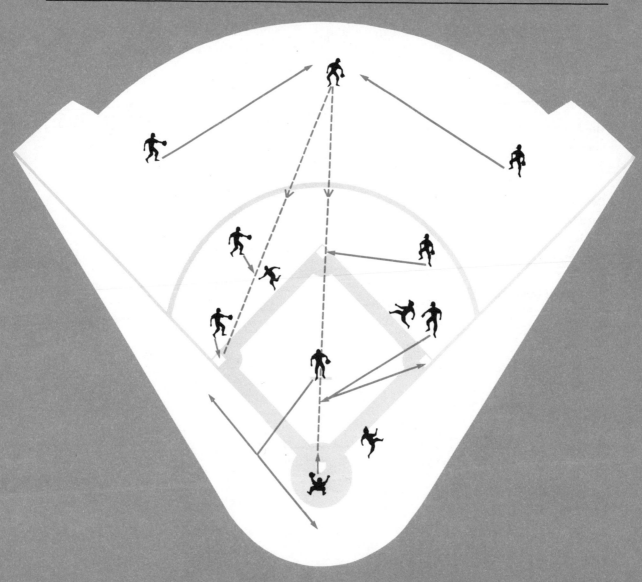

Basic objectives: the play at the plate and holding the baserunner from first to one base

With less than two outs, never let the tying or winning run go to third.

Center fielder: Field the ball and throw either to the plate, using the first baseman as a guide, or to third, using the shortstop as a guide.

Left and right fielders: Back up the center fielder.

First baseman: Move to the infield grass, directly in line with the center fielder and home plate. Following the catcher's instructions, (if the throw comes toward the plate), cut off the throw or let it through. If the throw goes to third, move back to first to cover first base.

Catcher: Cover home plate. If the throw comes toward the plate, prepare to take it, and instruct the first baseman whether or not to cut it off.

Pitcher: Move to a position outside the third base line, between third and home. Back up the base to which the throw goes—either home or third.

Shortstop: Move to the infield dirt, directly in line with the center fielder and third base. Following the third baseman's instructions (if the throw comes toward third), cut off the throw or let it through.

Third baseman: Cover third base. If the throw comes toward third, prepare to take it, and instruct the shortstop whether or not to cut it off.

Second baseman: Cover second base.

Note: The positions for this play combine those for two previous plays: 25 (single to center with a man on first), and 34 (single to center with a man on second).

38

Single to right with men on first and second (or with the bases loaded)

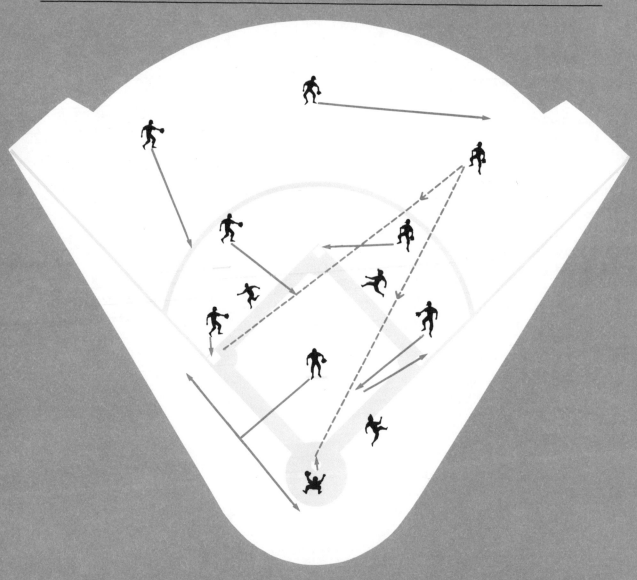

Basic objectives: the play at the plate or the play at third, and holding the batter to a single

Properly positioned cut-off men and accurate throws will keep the batter at first and still permit a tag play at home or third.

Right fielder: Field the ball, and throw either to the plate, using the first baseman as a guide, or to third, using the shortstop as a guide.

Center fielder: Back up the right fielder.

First baseman: Move to the infield grass, directly in line with the right fielder and home plate. Following the catcher's instructions (if the throw comes toward the plate), cut off the throw or let it through. If the throw goes to third, move back to first to cover the base.

Catcher: Cover home plate. If the throw comes toward the plate, prepare to take it, and instruct the first baseman whether or not to cut it off.

Pitcher: Move to a position outside the third base line between third and home. Back up the base to which the throw goes—either home or third.

Shortstop: Move to the infield grass, directly in line with the right fielder and third base. Following the third baseman's instructions (if the throw comes toward third), cut off the throw or let it through.

Third baseman: Cover third base. If the throw comes toward third, prepare to take it, and instruct the shortstop whether or not to cut it off.

Left fielder: Move toward third in case of a pickoff overthrow or rundown.

Second baseman: Cover second.

Note: The positions for this play combine those for two previous plays: 26 (single to right with a man on first), and 35 (single to right with a man on second).

FLY BALLS

39

Pop fly behind second base with no one on base (or with a man on third)

Basic objective: keeping all bases covered as the play is made

On all pop flies just beyond the infield, the outfielder closest to the ball should make the play if he can, calling off any infielders near the ball.

Center fielder: Catch the ball if possible. Yell to the infielders if you intend to make the play.

Shortstop and second baseman: Help on the pop fly. If the center fielder does not call for the ball, either of you can call for it and make the play. But remember that even after you have called for the ball, the center fielder can call you off.

Third baseman: Cover second base in case the ball drops and there is a play there.

Left and right fielders: Move toward the infield.

First baseman: Cover first base.

Pitcher: Cover third base.

Catcher: Cover home plate.

40

Pop fly behind second base with a man on first (or with men on first and third)

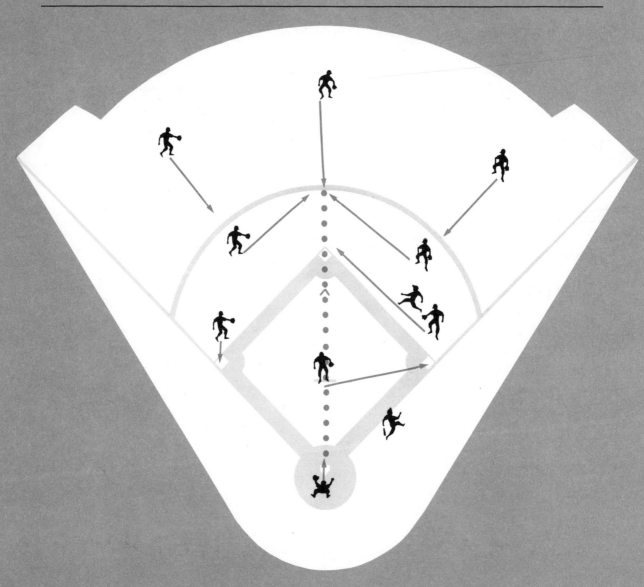

Basic objective: keeping all bases covered as the play is made

On all pop flies just beyond the infield, the outfielder closest to the ball should make the play if he can, calling off any infielders near the ball.

Center fielder: Catch the ball if possible. Yell to the infielders if you intend to make the play.

Shortstop and second baseman: Help on the pop fly. If the center fielder does not call for the ball, either of you can call for it and make the play. But remember that even after you have called for the ball, the center fielder can call you off.

Third baseman: Cover third base.

First baseman: Cover second base.

Left and right fielders: Move toward the infield.

Pitcher: Cover first base.

Catcher: Cover home plate.

Note: With a man on second, men on first and second, men on second and third, or with the bases loaded, the play is the same except that the pitcher leaves first base uncovered. Instead, he moves to a position outside the third base line between third and home, and if a throw comes to either base, he backs it up.

41

Possible sacrifice fly to left with a man on third

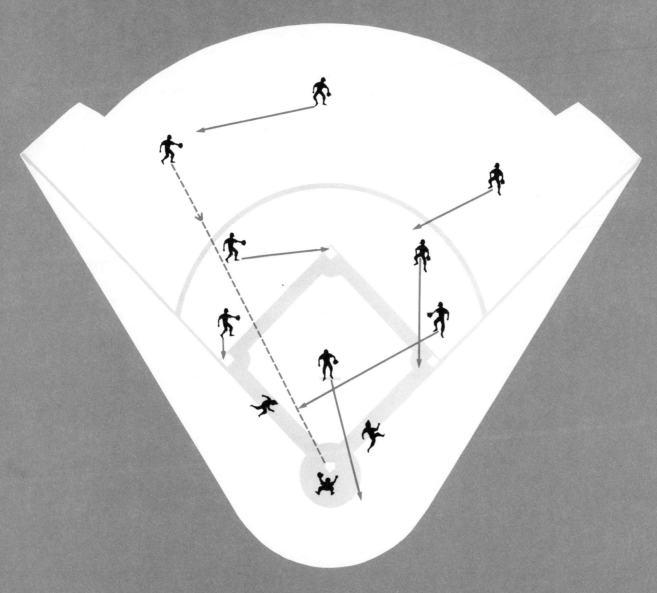

Basic objective: the play at the plate

On fly balls to the outfield with a man on third, the first baseman becomes the cut-off man.

Left fielder: Catch the ball, moving toward the plate if possible and, using the first baseman as a guide, throw home.

Center fielder: Back up the left fielder.

First baseman: Move to the infield grass, directly in line with the left fielder and home plate. Cut off the throw only if the runner from third turns around and goes back.

Catcher: Cover home plate and prepare to take the throw.

Pitcher: Back up home, keeping the plate on a line between you and the ball.

Third baseman: Cover third base.

Shortstop: Cover second base.

Right fielder: Back up second base in case the left fielder drops the ball and throws to second.

Second baseman: Cover first base.

42

Possible sacrifice fly to center with a man on third

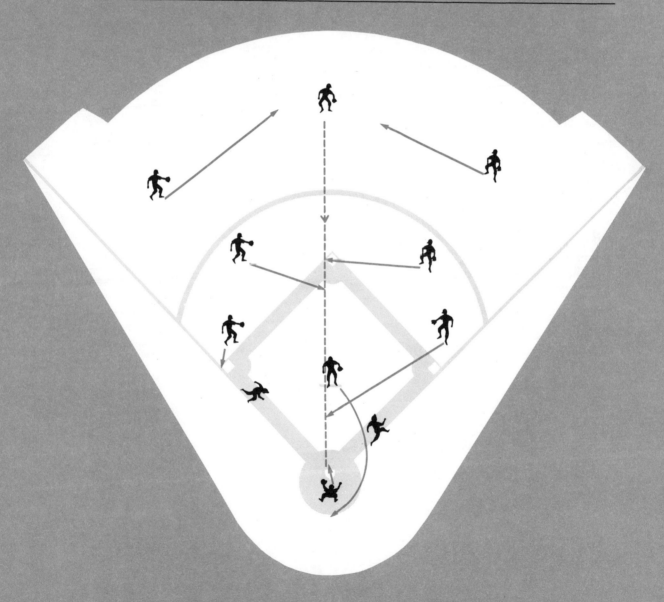

Basic objective: the play at the plate

On fly balls to the outfield with a man on third, the first baseman becomes the cut-off man.

Center fielder: Catch the ball, moving toward the plate if possible and, using the first baseman as a guide, throw home.

Left and right fielders: Back up the center fielder.

First baseman: Move to the infield grass, directly in line with the center fielder and home plate. Cut off the throw only if the runner from third turns around and goes back.

Catcher: Cover home plate and prepare to take the throw.

Pitcher: Back up home, keeping the plate on a line between you and the ball.

Third baseman: Cover third base.

Second baseman: Cover second base.

Shortstop: Back up second in case the center fielder drops the ball and has a play at second.

43

Possible sacrifice fly to right with a man on third

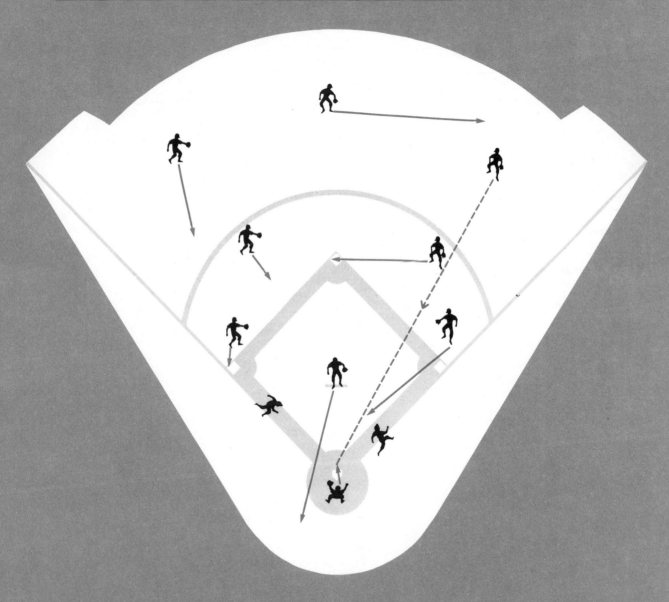

Basic objective: the play at the plate

On fly balls to the outfield with a man on third, the first baseman becomes the cut-off man.

Right fielder: Catch the ball, moving toward the plate if possible and, using the first baseman as a guide, throw home.

Center fielder: Back up the right fielder.

First baseman: Move to the infield grass, directly in line with the right fielder and home plate. Cut off the throw only if the runner from third turns around and goes back.

Catcher: Cover home plate and prepare to take the throw.

Pitcher: Back up home, keeping the plate on a line between you and the ball.

Third baseman: Cover third base.

Left fielder: Move toward third in case of a rundown.

Second baseman: Cover second base.

Shortstop: Back up second in case the right fielder drops the ball and has a play at second.

44

Possible sacrifice fly to left with men on first and third

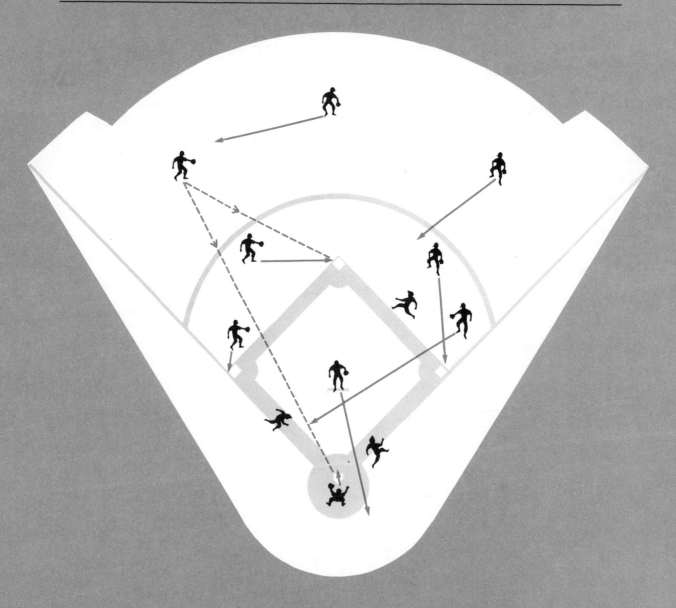

Basic objectives: the play at the plate and holding the other runner

An accurate throw and a properly positioned cut-off man will keep the runner on first from moving to second.

Left fielder: Catch the ball, moving toward the plate if possible and, using the first baseman as a guide, throw home. Or, if there is no play at home, throw to second.

Center fielder: Back up the left fielder.

First baseman: Move to the infield grass, directly in line with the left fielder and home plate. Following the catcher's instructions (if the throw comes toward the plate), cut off the throw or let it through.

Catcher: Cover home plate. If the throw comes toward the plate, prepare to take it, and instruct the first baseman whether or not to cut it off.

Pitcher: Back up home, keeping the plate on a line between you and the ball.

Shortstop: Cover second base, and take the throw if it comes there.

Right fielder: Back up second.

Third baseman: Cover third base.

Second baseman: Cover first base.

45

Possible sacrifice fly to center with men on first and third

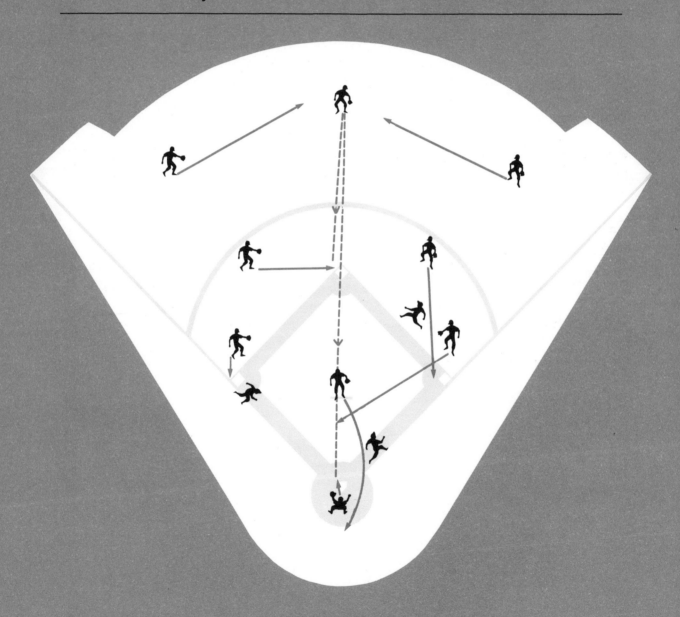

Basic objectives: the play at the plate and holding the other runner

98

An accurate throw and a properly positioned cut-off man will keep the runner on first from moving to second.

Center fielder: Catch the ball, moving toward the plate if possible and, using the first baseman as a guide, throw home. Or, if there is no play at home, throw to second.

Left and right fielders: Back up the center fielder.

First baseman: Move to the infield grass, directly in line with the center fielder and home plate. Following the catcher's instructions (if the throw comes toward the plate), cut off the throw or let it through.

Catcher: Cover home plate. If the throw comes toward the plate, prepare to take it, and instruct the first baseman whether or not to cut it off.

Pitcher: Back up home, keeping the plate on a line between you and the ball.

Shortstop: Cover second base, and take the throw if it comes there.

Third baseman: Cover third base.

Second baseman: Cover first base.

46

Possible sacrifice fly to right with men on first and third

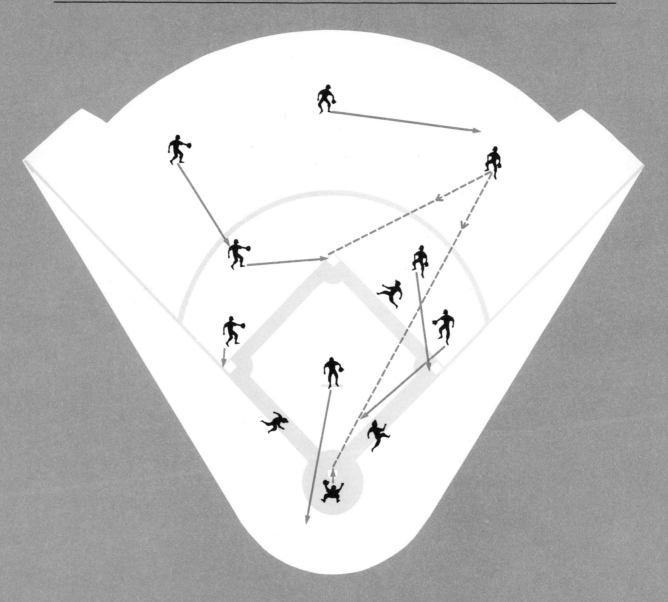

Basic objectives: the play at the plate and holding the other runner

An accurate throw and a properly positioned cut-off man will keep the runner on first from moving to second.

Right fielder: Catch the ball, moving toward the plate if possible and, using the first baseman as a guide, throw home. Or, if there is no play at home, throw to second.

Center fielder: Back up the right fielder.

First baseman: Move to the infield grass, directly in line with the right fielder and home plate. Following the catcher's instructions (if the throw comes toward the plate), cut off the throw or let it through.

Catcher: Cover home plate. If the throw comes toward the plate, prepare to take it, and instruct the first baseman whether or not to cut it off.

Pitcher: Back up home, keeping the plate on a line between you and the ball.

Shortstop: Cover second base, and take the throw if it comes there.

Left fielder: Move toward the infield in case of a rundown.

Third baseman: Cover third base.

Second baseman: Cover first base.

47

Possible sacrifice fly to left with men on second and third (or with the bases loaded)

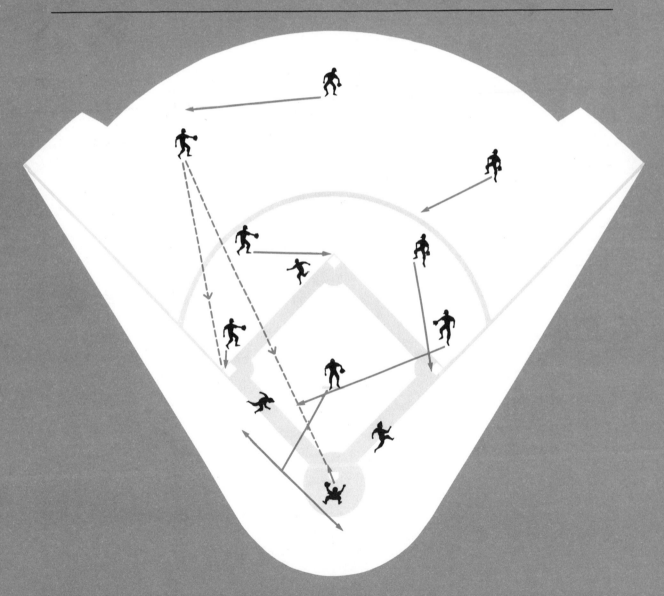

Basic objectives: the play at the plate and holding the other runner(s)

The man on second should not be able to advance if the throw goes home.

Left fielder: Catch the ball, moving toward the plate if possible and, using the first baseman as a guide, throw home. Or, if there is no play at home, throw to third.

Center fielder: Back up the left fielder.

First baseman: Move to the infield grass, directly in line with the left fielder and home plate. Following the catcher's instructions (if the throw comes toward the plate), cut off the throw or let it through.

Catcher: Cover home plate. If the throw comes toward the plate, prepare to take it, and instruct the first baseman whether or not to cut it off.

Pitcher: Move to a position outside the third base line near home plate and back up the base to which the throw goes—either home or third.

Third baseman: Cover third base and take the throw if it comes there.

Shortstop: Cover second base.

Second baseman: Cover first base.

Right fielder: Move toward second in case of a rundown.

48

Possible sacrifice fly to center with men on second and third (or with the bases loaded)

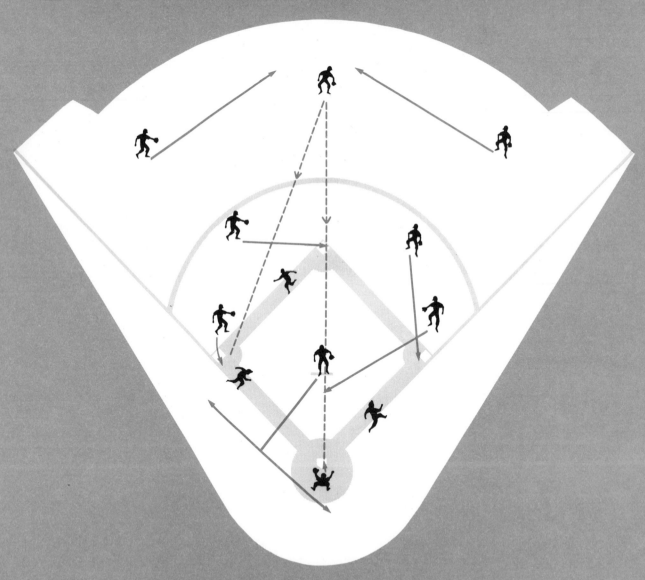

Basic objective: the play at the plate or holding the other runner(s)

For a play at the plate—successful or unsuccessful—the price is allowing an alert runner on second to move to third.

Center fielder: Catch the ball, moving toward the plate if possible and, using the first baseman as a guide, throw home. Or, if there is no play at home, throw to third.

Left and right fielders: Back up the center fielder.

First baseman: Move to the infield grass, directly in line with the center fielder and home plate. Following the catcher's instructions (if the throw comes toward the plate), cut off the throw or let it through.

Catcher: Cover home plate. If the throw comes toward the plate, prepare to take it, and instruct the first baseman whether or not to cut it off.

Pitcher: Move to a position outside the third base line, near home plate, and back up the base to which the throw goes—either third or home.

Third baseman: Cover third base and take the throw if it comes there.

Shortstop: Cover second base.

Second baseman: Cover first base.

49

Possible sacrifice fly to right with runners on second and third (or with the bases loaded)

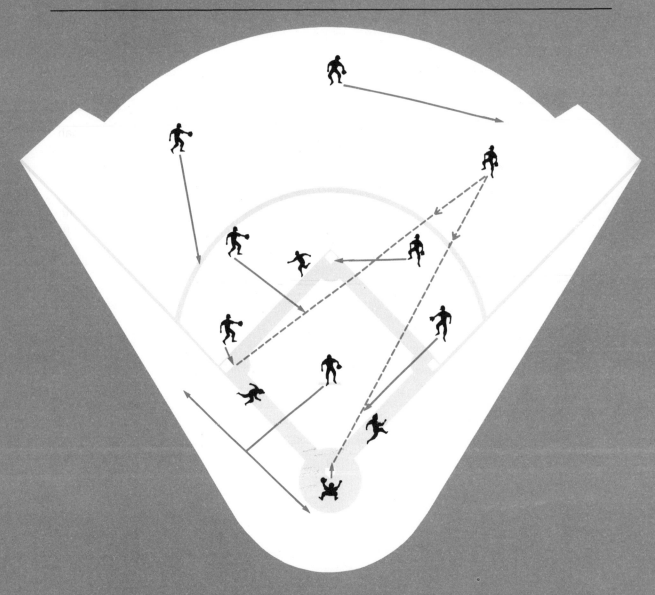

Basic objective: the play at the plate or the play at third

The throw home may be easier than the throw to third.

Right fielder: Catch the ball, moving toward the plate if possible and, using the first baseman as a guide, throw home. Or, if there is no play at home, throw to third.

Center fielder: Back up the right fielder.

First baseman: Move to the infield grass, directly in line with the right fielder and home plate. Following the catcher's instructions (if the throw comes toward the plate), cut off the throw or let it through.

Catcher: Cover home plate. If the throw comes toward the plate, prepare to take it, and instruct the first baseman whether or not to cut it off.

Pitcher: Move to a position outside the third base line between third and home and back up the base to which the throw goes—either third or home.

Left fielder: Move toward third in case of a rundown.

Shortstop: Move toward the infield grass to a position directly on a line with the right fielder and third base. Following the third baseman's instructions (if the throw comes toward third), cut off the throw or let it through.

Third baseman: Cover third base. If the throw comes toward third, prepare to take it, and instruct the shortstop whether or not to cut it off.

Second baseman: Cover second base.

Sacrifice bunt with a man on first

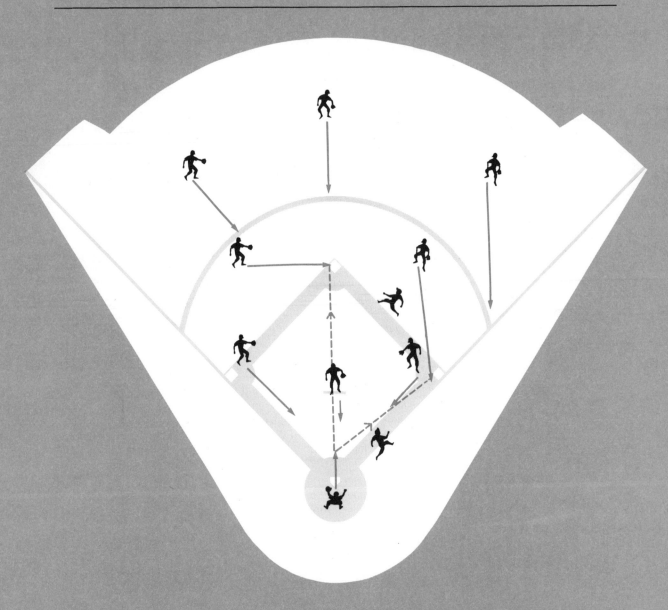

Basic objective: a force play at second or the sure out at first

The catcher calls the play.

Catcher: If possible, field the bunt and make the throw yourself—either to second or first. Or, instruct the infielder who fields the ball where to throw. If the third baseman fields the bunt, cover third.

Third baseman: Move in and cover the area between the third base line and the mound.

First baseman: Move in and cover the area between the first base line and the mound.

Pitcher: Break toward the plate after delivering the pitch.

Shortstop: Cover second base and take the throw if it comes there.

Center fielder: Back up second.

Left fielder: Move toward the infield in case of a rundown.

Second baseman: Cover first base and take the throw if it comes there.

Right fielder: Back up first base.

51A

Sacrifice bunt with men on first and second

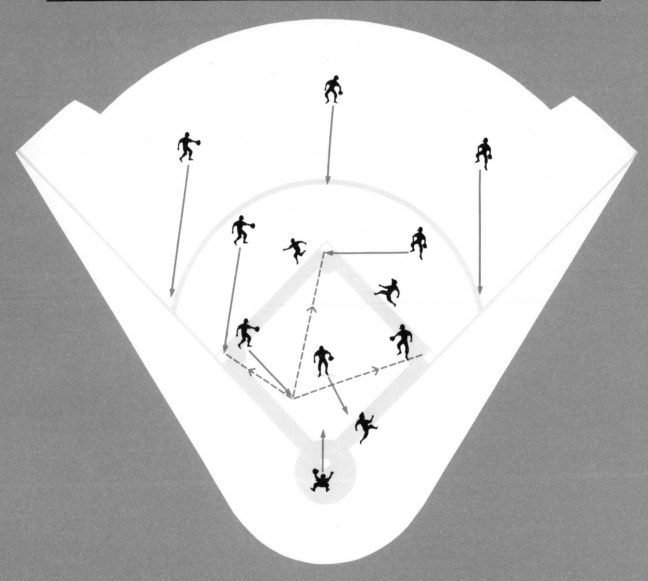

Basic objectives: the play at third, or the sure force out at second and a possible 'round-the-horn double play, or the sure out at first

The second baseman holds the runner close to second, allowing the shortstop to break directly to third.

Second baseman: While the pitcher sets, keep the runner at second close to the base. Then cover the base, and take the throw if it comes there.

Center fielder: Back up second.

Third baseman: Move in and cover the area between the third base line and the mound. If you field the ball (and it is likely you will), follow the catcher's instructions and throw to third, second, or first.

Catcher: Field the ball if it is near the plate. Otherwise, tell whoever fields it where to throw.

Pitcher: After delivering the pitch, cover the area between the mound and the first base line.

Shortstop: Cover third base and take the throw if it comes there.

Left fielder: Back up third.

First baseman: Cover first base, and take the throw if it comes there.

Right fielder: Back up first.

Notes: The ball will most often be bunted toward third because the offense usually assumes that if the third baseman fields the ball, third base will be left uncovered long enough for the runner from second to get there.

Executed properly, this is the defense that gives the fielders the most options in defending against the sacrifice bunt with runners on first and second. The third baseman has an easier throw to second or first and only a slightly more difficult throw to third than the pitcher would have if he fielded a bunt near the third base line. And the third baseman has the advantage of fielding a ball hit at him. The pitcher would usually have to run to catch up with a ball bunted down the third base line.

51B

Sacrifice bunt with men on first and second

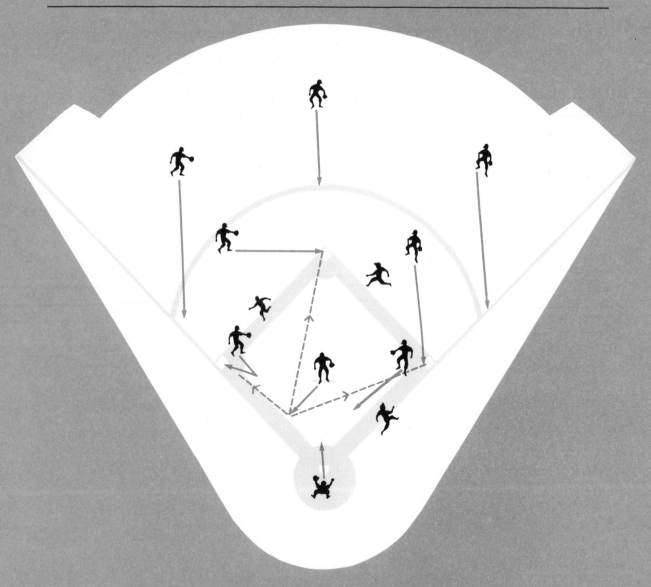

Basic objective: the play at third or the sure out at first (or possibly at second)

112

The pitcher should be in position to field a ball bunted toward third.

Pitcher: Break toward the third base line after delivering the ball. If you field the bunt (and it is likely you will), follow the catcher's instructions and throw to third, second, or first.

Catcher: Field the ball if it is near the plate. Otherwise, tell whoever fields it where to throw.

Third baseman: Move in slightly. If the ball is bunted past the pitcher, field it yourself and, following the catcher's instructions, throw to second or first. If the pitcher fields the bunt, or if the catcher does, move quickly back to third and take the throw if it comes there.

Left fielder: Back up third.

First baseman: Move in and cover the area between the first base line and the mound. Favor the mound area because the pitcher is moving away from it, leaving it poorly protected.

Shortstop: Cover second base and take the throw if it comes there.

Center fielder: Back up second.

Second baseman: Cover first base and take the throw if it comes there.

Right fielder: Back up first.

Notes: The ball will most often be bunted toward third because the offense usually assumes that if the third baseman fields the ball, third base will be left uncovered long enough for the runner from second to get there.
Because the pitcher has a difficult pivot and throw for a play at second, he will usually throw either to third or to first.

51C

Sacrifice bunt with men on first and second

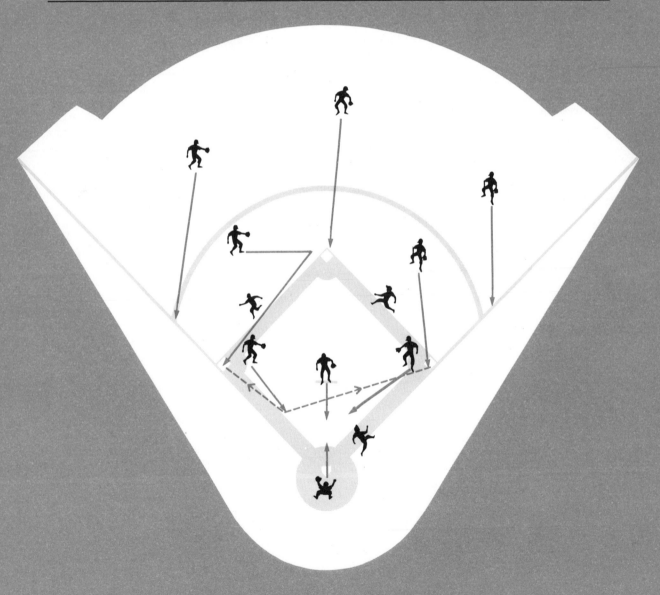

Basic objective: the play at third or the sure out at first

With three fielders charging the plate, the shortstop must both hold the runner close at second and cover third well before the runner gets there.

Shortstop: While the pitcher sets, keep the runner at second close to the base. When the pitcher begins his delivery, break to cover third and take the throw if it comes there.

Left fielder: Back up third.

Third baseman: Move in, and cover the area between the third base line and the mound. If you field the ball (and it is likely you will), throw to third or first, following the catcher's instructions.

Catcher: Field the ball if it is near the plate. Otherwise, tell whoever fields it where to throw—to either third or first.

Pitcher: After delivering the pitch, break toward the plate.

First baseman: Move in and cover the area between the first base line and the mound.

Second baseman: Cover first base and take the throw if it comes there.

Right fielder: Back up first.

Center fielder: Move toward second base, to cover it if possible.

Notes: The ball will most often be bunted toward third because the offense usually assumes that if the third baseman fields the ball, third base will be left uncovered long enough for the runner from second to get there.

Unless the center fielder plays very shallow, and thereby becomes in effect a fifth infielder, there will be no one covering second quickly enough for a force play there.

With three alternatives for defensing the sacrifice bunt when there are men on first and second, the defense must know which play is on. The manager signals his choice, usually to the catcher or the third baseman, and from there, the signal is relayed to the other fielders. Sometimes, the defense changes after every pitch, to confuse the batter and to try to catch the runners straying too far from their bases. (See pickoffs.)

SUCKER PLAYS

52

Double steal with men on first and third

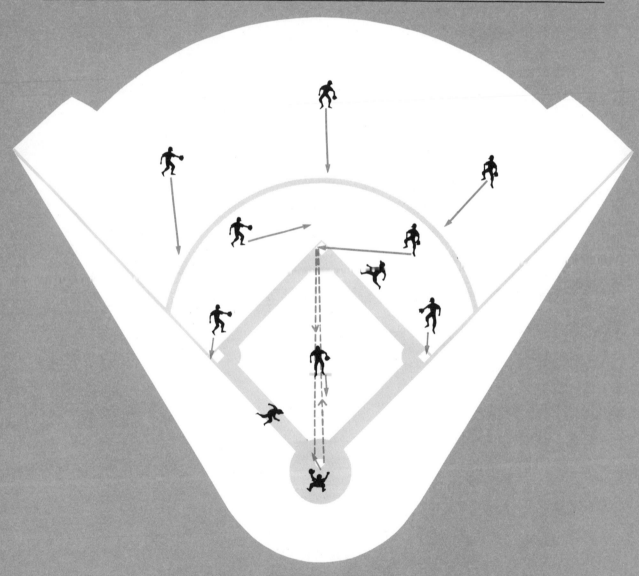

Basic objective: tagging the runner going to second without allowing the runner on third to score

Don't let the runner on third get a running start.

Catcher: Quickly look at the runner at third, freezing him. Then throw to second and cover the plate for a return throw.

Shortstop and second baseman: Decide beforehand who will cover second base. The man who covers the base takes the throw there and tags the runner, pursues him in a rundown, or throws home if the runner on third breaks for the plate. The other man backs up the play.

Pitcher: Be sure not to be in the way of the throw to second or a throw back to the plate.

Third baseman: Cover third base.

First baseman: Cover first base.

Outfielders: Move toward the infield in case of a rundown.

Notes: If the runner from first stops before reaching second or moves back toward first, and if the runner on third then breaks for the plate, the fielder taking the throw at second should throw home if there are less than two outs. The man between first and second can often be tagged before the runner on third reaches the plate, but that run will count unless there are already two outs.

An alternative to this play is for the catcher simply to throw back to the pitcher—a decoy throw. Instead of looking the runner back to third, the catcher tries to lure the runner on third into breaking for the plate. Or, the catcher can immediately throw to third, hoping to catch the runner leaning the wrong way. In either case, however, the defense concedes second to the runner on first.

53

Wild pitch or passed ball with men on first and third

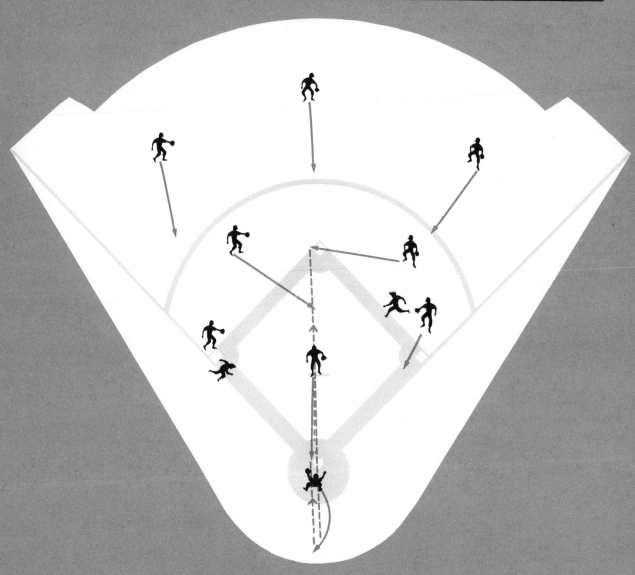

Basic objectives: the play at second and not permitting the runner on third to score

While the catcher moves after the ball, the cut-off man has time to get into position.

Catcher: Recover the ball. If the runner from third has broken for the plate, throw home. If the runner on third is holding but the runner on first has broken for second, throw to second, using the shortstop as a guide. *Don't* throw to second unless you are confident you can nail the runner.

Pitcher: Cover home plate and take the catcher's throw if it comes there. Be sure not to be in the way of a throw to second. If the catcher does throw to second, be prepared for a return throw to the plate.

Shortstop: Move to the infield grass near the mound, directly in line with the catcher and second base. If the catcher throws to second and the runner on third breaks for home, cut off the throw and throw home. Otherwise, let it through.

Second baseman: Cover second base. If the throw comes through, take it and tag the runner, pursue him in a rundown, or throw home if the runner on third breaks for home and there are less than two outs.

Center fielder: Back up second base.

Third baseman: Cover third base.

First baseman: Cover first base.

Left and right fielders: Move toward the infield in case of a rundown.

Notes: If there are less than two outs and the runner on third waits until the throw goes through to second base before breaking for home, the second baseman must throw home rather than pursuing the other baserunner in a rundown. (See note to play 52.)

The role of cut-off man in this play can be switched. If the second baseman is the cut-off man, the shortstop covers second. If the third baseman is the cut-off man, the shortstop covers third.

54

Foul pop-up to the third base side of home plate with men on first and third

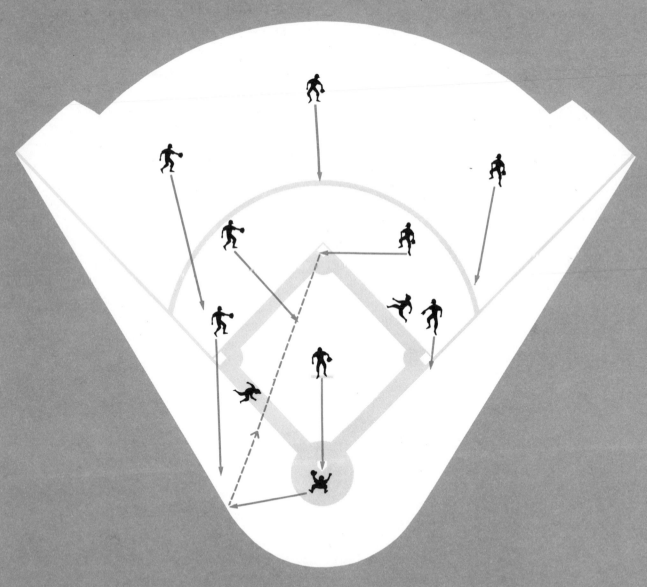

Basic objective: holding the runners

The runner on first will usually try only to draw a throw to second so that the runner from third can score.

Catcher: Catch the pop-up. If the man on first has tagged and broken for second, throw there, using the shortstop as a guide.

Third baseman: Help on the pop-up.

Shortstop: Move to the infield grass near the mound, directly in line with the catcher and second base. Cut off the catcher's throw unless the runner on third is holding and the runner from first is continuing toward second. If the runner on third has broken for the plate, throw home. If he is trapped off the base, run directly at him until he commits himself to a base, and then throw to that base.

Second baseman: Cover second base. If the throw comes through, take it and tag the runner, pursue him in a rundown, or throw home if the runner on third breaks for the plate and there are less than two outs. (See note to play 52.)

Center fielder: Back up second.

Left fielder: Move toward third base, to cover it if possible.

Pitcher: Cover home plate, and be prepared for a return throw.

First baseman: Cover first base.

Right fielder: Back up first.

55

Foul pop-up to the first base side of home plate with men on first and third

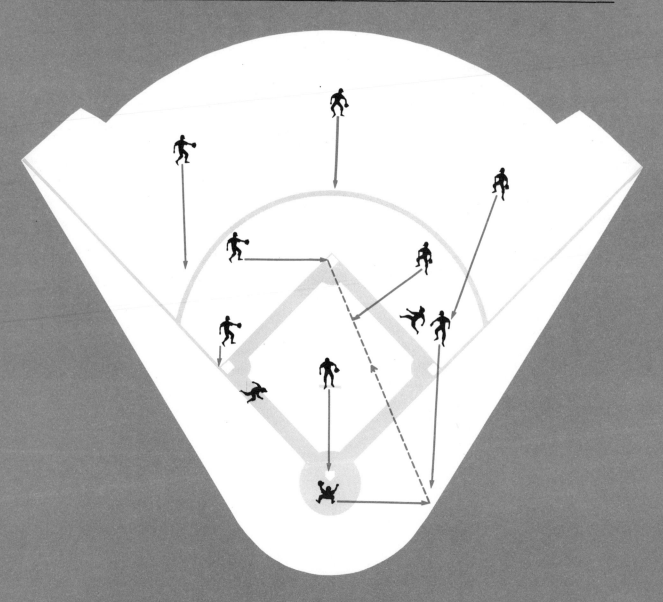

Basic objective: holding the runners

The runner on first will usually try only to draw a throw to second so that the runner from third can score.

Catcher: Catch the pop-up. If the man on first has tagged and broken for second, throw there, using the second baseman as a guide.

First baseman: Help on the pop-up.

Second baseman: Move to the infield grass near the mound, directly in line with the catcher and second base. Cut off the catcher's throw unless the runner on third is holding and the runner from first is continuing toward second. If the runner on third has broken for the plate, throw home. If he is trapped off the base, run directly at him until he commits himself to a base, and then throw to that base.

Shortstop: Cover second base. If the throw comes through, take it and tag the runner, pursue him in a rundown, or throw home if the runner on third breaks for the plate and there are less than two outs. (See note to play 52.)

Center fielder: Back up second.

Third baseman: Cover third base.

Left fielder: Back up third.

Pitcher: Cover home plate, and be prepared for a return throw.

Right fielder: Move toward first base, to cover it if possible.

56

Double steal with men on first and second

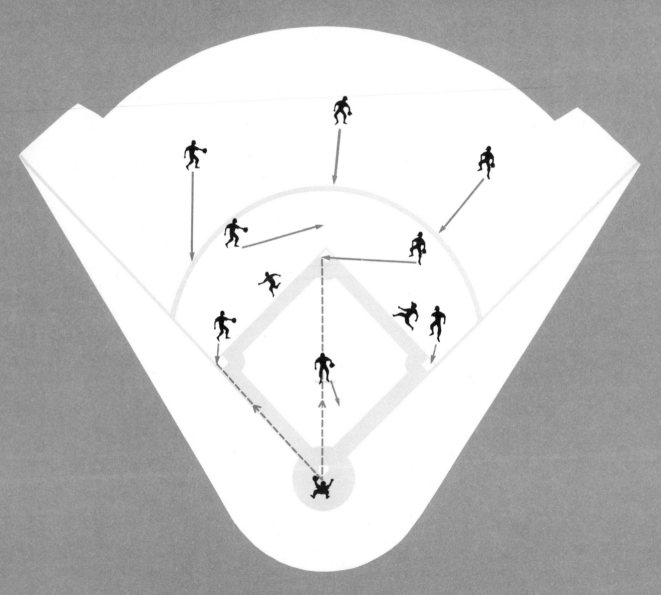

Basic objective: the play at third or the play at second

Usually the throw goes to third, but the runner going to second may be slow enough to warrant a throw there.

Catcher: Play for the surer out—to either third or second.

Third baseman: Cover third base and take the throw if it comes there.

Left fielder: Back up third.

Shortstop and second baseman: Decide beforehand who will cover second base. The man who covers takes the throw if it comes there. The other man backs up the play.

Center fielder: Move toward second in case of an overthrow.

Pitcher: Make sure not to be in the way of a possible throw to second.

First baseman: Cover first base.

Right fielder: Move toward the infield in case of a rundown.

PICKOFFS AND RUNDOWNS

The pickoff play at second

The second baseman, the shortstop, the pitcher, the catcher, or the manager can signal for the pickoff. After one man calls for the play, the affected players must relay the signal to one another. In addition it must be decided whether the shortstop or the second baseman will take the pickoff throw. With a right-handed batter, the second baseman may be closest to second and in a more convenient position than the shortstop to take the throw, but his movements are readily seen by the runner. The shortstop, on the other hand, usually plays behind the runner and is often watched only by the third base coach. The shortstop, therefore, may find it easier to move most quickly to the base without the runner being alerted.

If the pitcher originates the pickoff signal, he will signal the catcher, by kicking at the dirt, for example. The catcher must show the pitcher that he has received the signal, and he must relay it to the shortstop and the second baseman, specifying which man is to cover the base. Thus, the catcher might also kick the dirt but in the direction of either the shortstop or the second baseman. The designated man acknowledges the signal, and the pickoff play is on.

The play having been signaled, the pitcher stretches and, in his set position, watches the catcher. If the shortstop will take the throw, he waits until the runner has his biggest lead, and then moves two steps toward the runner. These steps shorten the distance between the shortstop and the base, but should not alert the third base coach to the pickoff if they are taken casually. They do, however, signal the catcher. When the shortstop does break for the base, the catcher opens his hand, signaling the pitcher that the shortstop is on his way. If the second baseman takes the throw, he also moves in a couple of steps before breaking for the bag. When the pitcher sees the catcher's signal, he whirls and throws to second.

The key to the play is split-second timing. The catcher must signal for the pitcher to throw precisely when the shortstop or second baseman is nearing the base. If the throw comes too early, there will be no one there. If it is too late, the runner will see the base being covered and realize the pickoff is coming.

The pickoff play at first base

When the first baseman is holding the runner at first, he is straddling the inside corner of the base, facing the pitcher. Because he needn't move to take a pickoff throw, the first baseman neither gives nor receives a pickoff signal. When he plays behind the runner, however, there must be a signal for the pickoff. The pitcher, the catcher, the first baseman, or the manager can initiate the signal. Perhaps the manager flashes the sign by picking up some dirt. The first baseman repeats the signal, acknowledging to the manager that he has received it and at the same time relaying it to the pitcher. The pitcher must then acknowledge the first baseman's sign, perhaps with a tug at the bill of his cap. The pickoff play is now on. As the pitcher sets, the first baseman breaks for first and takes the pickoff throw.

On a pickoff throw from the catcher, the first baseman and the catcher must exchange signs. Perhaps the catcher will initiate the play. He uses a signal different from the one for a pickoff throw by the pitcher. The first baseman acknowledges the signal also, perhaps with a tug at the cap, and the pickoff play is on. As he usually does when he is holding a runner on, the first baseman moves back a few steps toward his normal position when the pitcher begins his motion to the plate. Then, the first baseman moves quickly back to the bag as the catcher receives the pitch (often a pitchout) and pegs to first.

A variation of this pickoff play can be worked in a sacrifice bunt situation. Ordinarily, in a sacrifice bunt situation, the first baseman moves toward the plate as the pitcher sets, and first base is left unguarded until the second baseman arrives, after the pitch is delivered. On the pickoff play, the first baseman moves toward the plate while the pitcher sets, as if to defend against a bunt. Then he breaks back to the bag and takes the pitcher's throw. The play can be worked after a pitch on which the second baseman makes only a half-hearted attempt to cover first, encouraging the runner to move well off the base, even as the pitcher sets.

57A

Pickoff at second in a bunt situation with runners on first and second

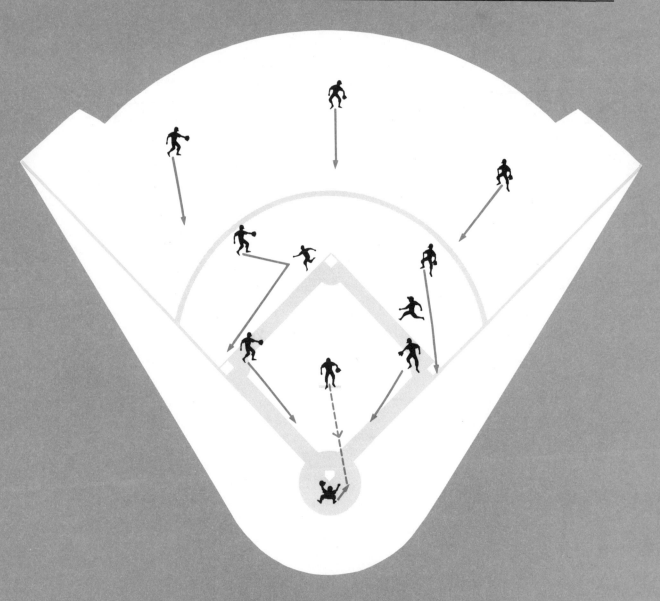

Basic objective: trapping the baserunner off second

The play takes place on two pitches. On the first pitch, the fielders defend against the bunt with no one covering second, hoping to make the baserunner at second believe that this will be the defense on subsequent pitches as well. The runner may then stray from the base and be picked off when the defense changes, on the next pitch.

ON THE FIRST PITCH

Pitcher: Pitch the ball well outside. The batter should not be able to bunt the ball, but in squaring around, he will verify that he does intend to bunt.

Shortstop: Bluff the runner back to second, then break to cover third while the pitcher is still in the set position.

Third baseman: Move in as if to cover the area between the mound and the third base line.

First baseman: Move in as if to cover the area between the mound and the first base line.

Second baseman: Cover first base.

Outfielders: Move toward the infield.

57B

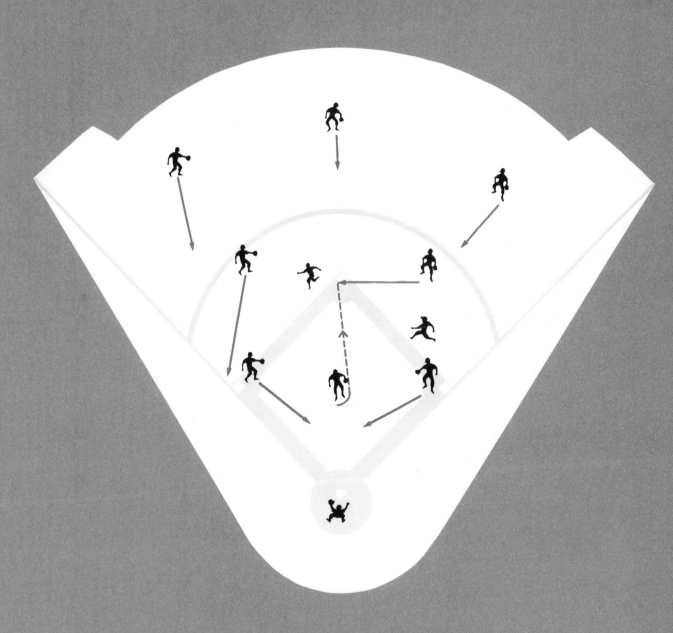

ON THE SECOND PITCH

Shortstop: Break directly for third as the pitcher sets.

Third baseman: Move in as if to cover the area between the mound and the third base line.

First baseman: Move in as if to cover the area between the mound and the first base line.

Second baseman: Wait until the shortstop breaks toward third and the runner moves as far off the base as he will go. Then break for second and take the pitcher's throw there.

Catcher: When the second baseman breaks for second, signal the pitcher by opening your bare hand.

Pitcher: Move to the set position. When the catcher signals, whirl and throw to second.

Outfielders: Move toward the infield.

The pickoff play at third base

The pitcher's pickoff throw to third is a rarely used play, but it is no more difficult than the pickoff at first with the first baseman playing behind the runner. The third baseman and the pitcher exchange signs. When the pitcher sets, the third baseman breaks to the base and takes a chest-high throw from the pitcher.

The pickoff throw from the catcher is somewhat more common, particularly in defending against a suspected squeeze. The catcher and the third baseman exchange signs. The third baseman moves quickly to the base as the catcher receives the pitch (often a pitchout) and pegs to third.

58

The rundown

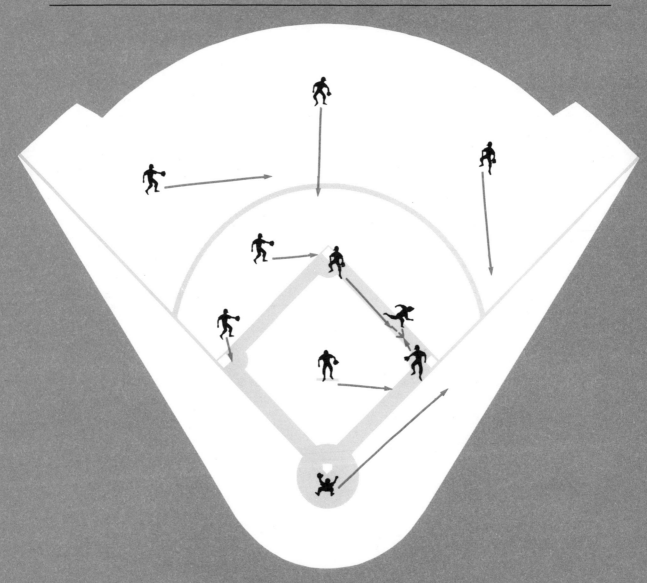

Basic objective: tagging the runner as quickly as possible, after one throw at most

The man who takes the pickoff throw usually becomes the run-down man, even if he moves the runner toward the next base.

Run-down man (the man with the ball): Keeping on the inside of the base line, run hard at the runner without faking a throw. If the runner is moving so quickly that you cannot tag him yourself, make an easy chest-high toss to the tag man when he moves toward the runner.

Tag man (the man between the runner and the base toward which the runner is moving): Stay in front of the base, inside the base line, until the runner is moving at full speed toward the base. Then break toward him. This is the signal to the run-down man to make the toss. Take the toss and tag the runner.

Notes: Any fielder who does not have the ball must make sure not to interfere with the runner.

A runner picked off so badly that he heads immediately for the next base can be a problem. The fielder who took the pickoff throw has to throw to the fielder who would ordinarily be the tag man but who now is closest to the runner. This fielder now either tags the runner or becomes the run-down man himself.

If a runner is caught midway between two bases and the run-down man has not yet taken the pickoff throw, the infielder holding the ball should run directly at the runner, make him commit himself to a base, and only then throw there. For example, after a tag play at second, a runner on third breaks for home, then changes his mind and stops, halfway down the line. The fielder holding the ball at second should run directly at the trapped runner, make the runner commit himself to a base, and then throw there.

59

Man on first picked off with men on first and third, (with men on first and second, or with the bases loaded)

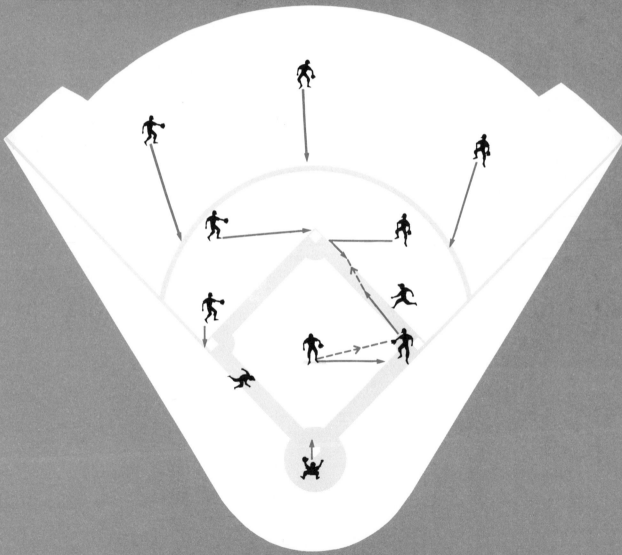

Basic objective: to tag the runner quickly, not allowing the other runner(s) to advance

The first baseman must decide whether he or the shortstop or second baseman will become the run-down man.

Pitcher: After throwing to first, back up first.

First baseman: Take the pitcher's throw. Become the run-down man, or if the runner is closer to second than first when you get the ball, throw to second, let the shortstop or second baseman move the runner back to first, and become the tag man.

Right fielder: Move toward first.

Shortstop or second baseman: Decide beforehand who will cover the base. The man who covers the base takes the first baseman's throw and becomes the tag man, or he becomes the rundown man, moving the runner back toward first. The other fielder backs up the man who takes the first baseman's throw, and covers the base if the runner is moved back toward first.

Center fielder: Move toward second.

Third baseman: Cover third base.

Left fielder: Move toward third.

Catcher: Cover home plate.

60

Man on second picked off with men on first and second, (with men on second and third or with the bases loaded)

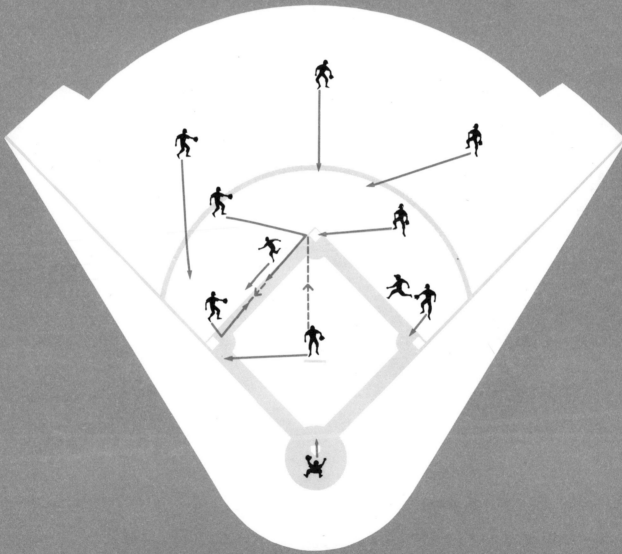

Basic objective: to tag the runner quickly, not allowing the other runner(s) to advance

The man who takes the pickoff throw must decide whether he or the third baseman will become the run-down man.

Pitcher: After throwing to second, back up third.

Shortstop or second baseman: Decide beforehand who will take the pitcher's throw at second. The man who takes the throw becomes the run-down man, moving the runner toward third. Or if the runner is closer to third than second when you get the ball, throw to third, let the third baseman move the runner back to second, and become the tag man. The man who does not take the pickoff throw at second backs up the play there and covers the base if the runner is moved toward third.

Center and right fielders: Move toward second.

Third baseman: Take the shortstop's or second baseman's throw and become the tag man, or become the run-down man, moving the runner back toward second.

Left fielder: Move toward third.

Catcher: Cover home plate.

First baseman: With a runner on first, cover the base. Otherwise, back up home.

Note: If there is a runner on first and he breaks for second while the third baseman is moving the runner toward second, a well-timed throw will nip the runner from first sliding into second and still leave the runner between second and third hung up.

61

Man on third picked off with the bases loaded, (with men on first and third, or with men on second and third)

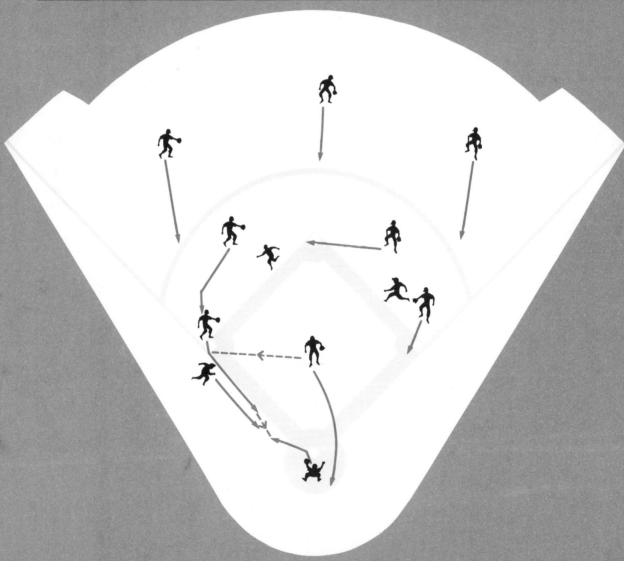

Basic objective: to tag the lead runner quickly, not allowing the other runner(s) to advance

The third baseman must decide whether he or the catcher will become the rundown man.

Pitcher: After throwing to third, back up home.

Third baseman: Take the pitcher's throw. Become the run-down man, or if the runner is closer to home than third when you get the ball, throw home, let the catcher move the runner back to third, and become the tag man.

Shortstop: Back up third.

Left fielder: Move toward third.

Catcher: Take the third baseman's throw and become the tag man, or become the run-down man, moving the runner back toward third.

Second baseman: Cover second base.

Center fielder: Back up second.

First baseman: With a runner on first, cover the base. Otherwise, move toward home.

Right fielder: Back up first.

Note: If there is a runner on second and he breaks for third while the catcher is moving the runner toward third, a well-timed throw will nip the runner from second sliding into third and still leave the runner between third and home hung up.

OFFENSE

HITTING

On the bench

When his team is at bat, the player starts his work even before he steps to the plate. He should be carefully observing the other team for any weakness. Sometimes, after the catcher has given the sign, a pitcher or an infielder (especially the shortstop and second baseman) may give away the sign by readying himself for a certain pitch. He may, for instance, crouch down for a curve or straighten slightly when a fastball is to be delivered. Players on the bench should be especially alert to what kind of pickoff move the pitcher has. Outfielders should be studied—whether they are right- or left-handed, how powerful their throwing arms are, etc.

On deck

Similarly, the batter can help himself and his team in the on-deck circle. He should think about the situation in which he'll be batting, considering such factors as the number of outs there may be, the men on base and their positions, and the defensive alignment—will the infield be in or back, will the outfield be pulled to either side. All these factors will influence his behavior at bat. The man on deck should be thinking of how this particular pitcher has pitched to him in the past, particularly what weaknesses he has exploited.

The player on deck can also assist his team when there are men on base. For example, he should indicate whether a runner coming to the plate should slide or not, and he should be alert to any of the catcher's misplays. In the event of a play at the plate, he should get the mask and bat out of the way and stand on the first base side of the plate, so that the runner can see him signaling whether to remain standing or to slide. (It is important that he signal rather than shout, since crowd noise may drown out verbal instructions.)

General batting strategy

General batting strategy early in the game is to try to score as many runs as possible by having batters hit away, and in the late innings, if the game is close, to rely more on moving every man into scoring position, even at the expense of an out. In other words, play for the big inning early; sacrifice later. But obviously, not every team can play by the book. Some teams, without the power to go for the big inning, have to scratch out every run, relying on good pitching and defense to keep the other team's score down. As far as overall batting strategy goes then, each manager must make his own decision according to the particular team he's working with.

The batting order

It's common sense to put the best hitters up first in the lineup. Thus, these players will bat more often, and the probability of greater scoring increases.

The lead-off batter should be a man who can get on base. It is not important that he be a power hitter, but he should have a good eye and should not be a man who strikes out often.

The second batter should be able to bunt well, for he will often be called upon to sacrifice. He should also be the sort of batter who can hit to right field for hit-and-run plays.

The third batter should be the man on the team who gets hits most consistently. If possible, he should be a fast man, able to avoid double plays.

The fourth batter, or clean-up man, should be a power hitter, able to move the men around the bases.

The fifth batter will also hit in situations with runners in scoring position.

Since he will often lead off the inning, the sixth batter should have basically the same abilities as the first man in the order. However, since it is more likely that he will come to bat with men on base, he should have power too.

The seventh man should be a good bunter, and a fairly good hitter to right.

Since he will be batting ahead of the pitcher, the eighth batter should be fast, making it easier, after he reaches base, for the pitcher to sacrifice bunt. If possible, he should be able to avoid hitting into a double play so that the pitcher won't lead off the next inning.

The ninth batter will be the weakest hitter, almost invariably the pitcher.

Taking the sign

In most cases the batter will look to the third base coach for a sign before stepping to the plate for the pitch. In order to confuse the opposition, it is important that the coach give a series of decoy signals before and after he gives the real sign. It is equally important for the batter, once he has received the sign, not to turn away immediately to take his batting position. He should continue to watch the coach until all signs have been given, again to ensure that the opposition will not be able to pick up the sign.

At the plate

There is no right way to bat. Each player will adopt the method of batting that best suits him. But there are certain fundamentals. A good batter must know the strike zone. This may seem self-evident, but it is remarkable how many hitters ignore the strike zone. Not only is the hitter likely to miss the ball, but the pitcher will be quick to note the mistake and offer a similarly tempting but difficult-to-hit pitch the next time. A good pitcher won't pitch to the strike zone unless the batter forces him to.

Pitches to the inside of the plate should generally be pulled; those to the outside, hit to the opposite field. The game situation and the position of the outfielders will dictate whether the batter should attempt to pull the ball or go to the opposite field.

Outguessing the pitcher

Because of the incredible speed of today's pitchers, many batters feel that they must try to outguess the pitcher—to expect a certain pitch and set themselves to act accordingly—in order to hit the ball. Many authorities hold that a player should anticipate a fastball and adjust to the curve, on the theory that it's easier to slow down reactions than to speed them up. They believe that if the batter anticipates a breaking ball and a fastball is delivered, he won't be able to correct himself and hit the ball in time. Some players believe just the opposite, though. These players have more than likely had the embarrassing experience of swinging at a ball that hasn't even reached the plate yet; they were looking for a fast one when the pitcher changed up.

Some players decide which sort of pitch they're going to swing on, and then swing only if this is delivered. Generally speaking, these batters look for a pitch in a certain area. If a batter hits the high inside pitch well, he will set himself for such a pitch and, if it is delivered, swing at it whether it is a fastball or a breaking pitch.

All this preplanning involves knowing what the pitcher is going to throw before he throws it, which is often the result of observing any patterns of a certain pitcher (or catcher), such as the pitches he uses in certain situations. There is no substitute, however, for the ability to wait until the last second and react to whatever pitch is thrown. Outguessing the pitcher is a shortcut that should be allowed only when the batter is in no danger of striking out.

(There are even some batters who, in their battle with the pitcher, will deliberately swing and miss on a pitch they like in order to lure the pitcher into giving them that pitch again, perhaps later in the game when a hit will be crucial.)

Taking the first strike

In general, the batter takes the first strike when:
- the opposition is far ahead
- the previous batter has hit the first pitch for an out
- the pitcher has control trouble
- the count is three and nothing

However, the batter should attempt to hit the first good strike when runners are in scoring position and the runs will increase the lead, break a tie, or make the score close. Sometimes it's good to swing away when the sacrifice is expected, since the defense will be out of position and the chances of hitting through the infield are better.

Unless the batter is the potential tying or winning run, it isn't wise to swing at a questionable pitch with less than two strikes. In general the batter should attempt to hit *his* pitch, not the pitcher's, which is likely to be at the edges of the strike zone.

Varying the swing

Different situations require different strokes. (The extreme example of this, covered later, is the bunt.) When the infield is in, simply meeting the ball so as to hit past the infielders but in front of the outfielders, may be more effective than swinging from the heels. With two outs and no one on base, however, the batter should swing hard, simply because if he manages more than a single, he puts himself in scoring position immediately. Just a single may be of no use if the man following him is not a good long-ball hitter.

Other game situations calling for variation in the stroke include:
- a runner on third and less than two out. Here the batter should look for a high pitch that he can hit deep to the outfield, allowing the runner ample time to tag up and score after the catch.
- a runner on second and no one out. In this situation it's best to hit a grounder to the right side, moving the runner to third so that he can score on a long fly.

- and, of course, after two strikes, batters should cut down on the swing in most situations, to avoid a strikeout.

Hitting behind the runner

The ability to hit the ball behind the baserunner is rare and beautiful. This skill is invaluable in situations that demand the execution of the hit-and-run play but is also quite useful on other occasions. For example, for a right-handed batter it's good to try to hit behind the runner with a man on first and less than two outs. The second baseman will be playing close to second and will have to move to the left to catch the ball. Thus, he will have difficulty making the force play at second.

If successful, hitting behind the runner on first results in runners on first and third. Of course, pitchers anticipating this tactic will attempt to defeat it by throwing inside to right-handers and outside to left-handers.

If the count reaches two and nothing, the pitcher is in a hole and may decide simply to get the ball over the plate. Here the batter can take the initiative and either hit behind the runner or swing away at what is likely to be a fat pitch.

The hit-and-run play

The elements of daring, split-second timing, and skill necessary to the successful execution of this play make it one of the most exciting sights in baseball. In essence it is a quasi-sacrifice play, undertaken to break up the double play. In the play the runner (usually on first) breaks for the next base as the pitcher starts his delivery, and the batter hits the pitch behind the runner.

The purpose of the hit-and-run play is usually a defensive one—to eliminate the double play. With a slow runner on first or at the plate, it may make good sense to use this play as such a defensive tactic, but the hit-and-run can also be an offensive play. It can advance a runner from first to third on a single that would normally get him only to second. The defense against the play is the pitchout, in which the catcher signals for the pitchout and throws out the man dashing for second.

The play is a gamble, so it is usually attempted when the team at bat is ahead or when the score is tied. In addition it is best attempted when the batter is ahead or even on the count. In these situations the pitcher wants to get the ball over the plate and is less likely to throw any fancy stuff, much less a pitchout.

A three-and-one pitch is a natural for the hit-and-run, since there is no danger of a pitchout and the batter can safely assume he will have a good pitch to hit. If he doesn't, it's ball four of course, and there is nothing lost in starting the baserunner.

Often the element essential to a successful hit-and-run is surprise. If the defense knows that the play is on, the runner is a sitting duck. The other essential factor to a successful execution of the play is simply that the batter hit the ball. Once it has been signaled that the batter is going to be hitting the next pitch, the baserunner will be on the move with the pitch. If the batter fails to get a piece of that pitch, the runner will probably be thrown out.

To work the hit-and-run best, the batter has to do more than just hit the ball—he has to hit it through a hole in the infield. Therefore he should know in advance who will be covering second base. In general the shortstop covers for left-handed batters and the second baseman for right-handers. So the left-handed batter will be trying to put the ball through the shortstop's position, and the right-handed batter will try to hit through the second baseman's spot. Since the first baseman will probably be playing closer than usual to the bag in order to hold the runner, the hole on the right side of the infield will be larger. This, and the fact that double plays are more easily begun from the left side of the infield than from the right side, makes the play easier for right-handed batters. Of course, the batter should be able to hit to either side of the field, in case the defense upsets the expected order of things, for example, by having the shortstop cover second for a right-handed batter. But no batter can decide *after* the ball has been delivered and the defense has committed itself where he will hit. The batter can only make an educated guess, execute correctly, and hope for the best.

The play is usually best attempted with one out. With no outs there are probably safer ways—hitting away, a sacrifice—of advancing the runner.

With men on first and third, the hit-and-run is sometimes attempted; with a runner on second, or runners on second and third, it is rarely tried. In the latter case, the third baseman is close to third, leaving a weakness on that side more easily exploited by a right-handed batter.

The worst thing that can happen on a hit-and-run is for the ball to be lined to an infielder, thus resulting in the very thing that the tactic is designed to prevent—a double play. On a regular fly ball the runner will be able to retrace his steps and return to his base in time.

The run-and-hit play

According to some, the hit-and run should actually be called the run-and-hit play, since the runner breaks before the batter hits the ball. But the run-and-hit play is distinct from the hit-and-run. In the run-and-hit, the batter usually hits away, if he gets a pitch he likes, in whatever direction he can. Otherwise, the play is a simple steal, initiated by the manager or coach on a pitch he feels will be over the plate. This is usually a three-and-one or a three-and-two pitch. As in the hit-and-run, the reasoning behind the play is that if the next pitch is a ball, the runner on first will advance anyway.

Essential to the success of this play is a strong hitter. With a power hitter at bat, the run-and-hit is a better choice than the hit-and-run. Again, as with the hit-and-run, the element of chance in the play makes it a foolish choice when the offense is far behind.

Bunting

There are two general categories of bunts—the sacrifice bunt and the bunt for a base hit. In the sacrifice bunt, the offense incurs an out in order to advance a runner; in the bunt for a base hit, the batter attempts to reach first base by bunting against a defense that isn't expecting the play.

In a sacrifice bunt, the batter faces the pitcher by squaring around and "catching" the ball on the bat. Placement of the bunt will vary with the game situation (how many men on which bases, etc.), but the important thing in a sacrifice bunt is for the ball to be bunted into fair territory.

If the manager is employing the big-inning strategy, he won't want to sacrifice. The sacrifice is usually initiated with a man on first or a man on second, or with men on first and second, and less than two strikes on the man at bat. (If the pitch is fouled on the third strike, it's an automatic out.) The play is generally used when the game is close—to tie a score, break a tie, or increase a slight lead on a subsequent single or long fly. In general, it is attempted with a weak hitter, often the pitcher, at bat.

It is not wise to sacrifice with the bottom half of the batting order coming up to bat, since the purpose of the sacrifice is to move a man into a position from which he can score on a single or on a long fly, and the bottom of the order is less likely to deliver.

The defense will often be expecting a bunt in sacrifice situations, so the batter must note the position of the infielders and place the ball accordingly. If the batter is trying to advance a runner from first to second, he should bunt the ball to a position between the mound and either of the base lines. A bunt toward first in this situation is good, since the first baseman must stay on the bag until the pitcher starts his delivery. If the bunt is to advance runners from first and second, the bunt generally should be made to a point three or four feet from the third base line and far from the plate. The ball is placed along the line so that the third baseman will have to field it and leave third uncovered. Or the bunt can be pushed toward the first base line.

The pitcher expecting a bunt will usually throw high inside pitches, which are hard to bunt on the ground. To keep from popping up, the batter must stand fairly erect and hit down on the ball.

Sometimes in a bunt situation, a good batter can take advantage of the defense's expectations and quickly slide his hand back down the bat handle to try to chop the ball through the infield. But this requires a lot of skill. Frivolously attempted, it will more likely result in a double play or strikeout than a base hit.

The squeeze play

With a runner on third, any bunt is a squeeze play. The runner can wait until the ball is bunted before trying to score (the safety squeeze); he can break for the plate as the pitcher is about to deliver the ball (the semisuicide squeeze); or he can begin his dash when the pitcher winds up (the suicide squeeze).

The safety squeeze can only be attempted with the infielders playing back, not expecting a bunt. The offense must do nothing to tip off the play. The runner takes only a normal lead off third, and the batter doesn't square around too early. The runner is not obliged to break for the plate unless the bunt is well placed.

With the infield in, the offense is forced to try either a semisuicide or a suicide squeeze. In the semisuicide squeeze, the runner on third breaks for the plate when it's too late for the pitcher to stop or alter his delivery. If the runner is fast and times his break properly, the batter needs only to bunt the ball properly, and the infielders will have little chance for the play at the plate. This play is best attempted when the batter is ahead of the pitcher on the count and the pitcher has to get the ball over. The essence of this play is for the runner to make his break only as the ball is about to leave the pitcher's hand.

In the suicide squeeze, the runner on third breaks for the plate too late for the pitcher to stop his delivery but early enough for him to change the pitch. The runner takes the additional risk for the sake of the better jump he gets. When the pitcher sees the runner breaking for the plate, he's going to throw a pitch that will spin the batter out of the box—a pitch directed straight at his head. It takes an awfully resourceful batter to bunt a pitch like this. Clearly the suicide squeeze is the biggest gamble of any squeeze play. But any squeeze play has an element of gambling and should only be attempted when the offense needs the run very badly, and/or the man at the plate has a habit of striking out.

Bunt for a hit

With an exceptionally fast runner at the plate and an unsuspecting defense, the manager may want to call for a bunt for a base hit. Left-handers employ a drag bunt; right-handers push or punch the ball. The bunt is often made to the right side of the infield when the first baseman is playing deep. The bunt itself should be past the pitcher, forcing the first baseman to field the ball and throw to the pitcher covering first. A bunt to the left side of the infield is easier to defend, since the first baseman will not have to leave his bag and will be waiting for the throw. Surprise and speed are the essential ingredients to this play.

RUNNING

On the bases

The key to good baserunning is judgment, not speed. Speed is helpful, of course, but not essential. Maury Wills was a great baserunner not because of his speed (there were players on his team who were faster), but because of his ability to outthink the opposition.

Strategy on the base paths is determined by the game situation. The runner should ask himself if the result of his action will be worth the risk; if his team can't afford the out, he has to be very careful.

The number of outs in an inning often moderates a baserunner's aggressiveness. With no outs runners should play it safe and only advance on a sure hit. With one or two outs, the importance of getting a man into scoring position at second may justify the risk of a steal. With two outs it is especially important that a runner be in scoring position, but there is usually no point in risking an out by trying to steal third. However, with one out, the greater chance of scoring from third may justify a speedy runner's steal attempt from second.

Running from the batter's box on a batted ball

The first rule is to run hard. Even if it looks as if the defense will have no trouble making the out, there's always the possibility of an error. This consideration applies to all baserunning situations.

On a ball hit to the infield, the batter should run hard with an even stride to a point five yards past first. It may help for the runner to think of this point as his goal, forcing himself to run through first at full speed. After hitting first, the runner should slow down gradually to prevent pulled muscles. If the throw to first is wild, the runner should listen to the first base coach for instructions on whether to try for second.

When the ball is hit to the outfield, the runner should make the turn at first as if for an extra-base hit and should be prepared to go to second if he can. He should approach first on the outside of the base line, touch the inside of the base with his left foot, make a pivotlike turn at the base, and proceed toward second in a straight line.

Touching any base with the inside, or left, foot is better than stepping on the base with the right foot for two reasons: first, the runner gets a stronger push off the bag, and second, he tends to take a more direct line to the next base. However, it is not vital that he touch the base with his left foot, and he should never break stride or slow down in an attempt to do so.

Wide turns waste time, but extra-sharp turns are dangerous. On a hit to center or left field, the runner can round first and move farther toward second than on a hit to right. He can also make a wider turn on a ball thrown to third or the plate from left or center field than on a ball thrown from right field to second base. (In the latter situation, sometimes a fake toward second will draw a throw and maybe an error.) When the throw goes to third or to the plate, the defense may cut off the ball and make the play for the batter if he rounds his base too far.

Good baserunning is a learned skill. Beginning players must conquer the strong impulse to run on any hit. Any man on base should have a clear picture of the game situation. He should know where the ball is at all times, how many are out, what the pitcher's pickoff move is, how the outfielders and infielders are playing the batter. All these, and many other factors, will govern his baserunning behavior.

Stealing

The key to a successful steal is to get a good jump on the pitcher. Opinions about the correct distance of the lead vary; three-and-a-half steps, two steps and a slide, two-and-a-half steps and a dive, etc. Hard and fast rules are of little use, though. The correct distance of the lead will depend on a variety of factors, the ability and speed of the base-runner paramount among them.

There are two schools of thought on the method for taking the lead. Some feel that in moving off the base the runner should keep his feet from crossing, lest the pitcher's throw to the base catch him in this awkward position. Others claim that the method of not crossing the feet leads to a skipping motion that is even more vulnerable to a pickoff. They recommend instead that in moving off first the runner should bring his left foot behind his right on the first step, then his right foot past his left on the second. Even if the pitcher throws to first while the runner has his legs crossed, the runner is in a good position to pivot for the dive back to the base.

Whatever method the runner chooses, he should not start his lead until the pitcher is on the rubber. Since the pitcher is not permitted to take his stance on the rubber without the ball, this guards against any hidden ball trick. And with the pitcher on the rubber, he cannot attempt a pickoff without stepping toward the base.

It is axiomatic that the runner steals on the pitcher, not the catcher. It is against the pitcher that he takes his lead and, most important, against him that he gets his start toward second—his "jump." Without a good jump on the pitcher, the runner can be thrown out even by a weak throw from the catcher.

Before trying to steal on any pitcher, the runner must know when he can; that is, he must know that pitcher's move for the pickoff. If he hasn't already observed the pickoff move, a good tactic is to try to draw the throw. He takes a rather long lead but with his weight on the left foot, facilitating a quick return to the bag. Most pitchers, especially right-handers, give away their intentions with certain body movements. Left-handers are harder to steal on because their moves to first are quite similar to their moves toward the plate. However, any pitcher has to bend his front knee slightly to deliver the pitch. Also, the movement of the front foot differs in pitching. Some pitchers may lean at the start of the pitch or use a high leg motion; others may turn their bodies slightly toward the base before attempting to pick off the runner.

Runners should never telegraph their intention to steal or fake a steal. If a runner wishes to place his weight unequally, he must disguise the fact. Weight should at least look as though it's evenly distributed. If the pitcher can tell that the runner's weight is on his right foot, he can more easily pick him off. The hands should be *off* the knees. Left on, they'll have to be removed before running, thus wasting precious time.

Once the runner has learned the pitcher's move and after he has looked for the coach's sign so that he knows what the batter will be doing on the pitch, he is ready to make his break. Once he breaks, he can't change his mind. He starts as the pitcher goes into his motion to the plate, making a quick pivot on his right foot, crossing over with the left foot. His body, low to start, like a sprinter's, gradually becomes more erect as he runs. He always slides into the next base. The type of slide will depend on the situation. If the throw is expected to go to one side of the bag, a hook or fade-away slide can be made. This is made to the side of the bag opposite the fielder. On a hook slide, the foot catches the bag; on a fade-away, the hand touches it. A pull-up slide is generally faster but offers the fielder more body area to tag and so is generally reserved for when the base is clearly stolen and the runner may want to advance farther. On any slide the runner comes in with spikes and hands off the ground to avoid injury.

Stealing third

The same basic rules apply here as in the steal from first except that the lead can be a little longer—four-and-a-half steps, possibly—since the infielder does not play on the bag. Stealing third is better attempted with a right-hander at the plate because he blocks the catcher's view and may even obstruct his throw. A successful pickoff is less likely, since the pitcher and a moving second baseman or shortstop must synchronize their movements to make the play. And the third base coach will be warning the runner should a fielder move toward the bag.

Stealing home

This play is almost impossible, and the opposition rarely expects it. For this very rea-

154

son, it is sometimes successful. A fake or two before the actual attempt will strengthen the impression that the runner is simply playing, trying to rattle the pitcher. The runner, sliding into home, hopes that the catcher will have trouble both catching the pitch and tagging him. Still, stealing home is a desperation move, rarely seen in the major leagues.

Delayed steal

On this play the rule of stealing on the pitcher is ignored. The runner moves as if to go back to first, then breaks for second as the catcher raises his arm to throw back to the pitcher. If no one is covering second, the catcher is forced to wait for the fielder to cover before he can make his throw. The farther the man covering second is from the bag, the better the chances of success on this play.

Fake steal

A fake steal is often a good way to worry the defense. It is done with two or three quick steps as the pitcher starts his delivery. It can draw the infield out of position, show the runner and batter who will be covering second on a steal, or uncover the pitchout defense. It's a useful maneuver if the hit-and-run is contemplated since it will show the batter where the holes will be.

When to steal

Every steal is a gamble. When there are two outs, it's advisable to make the attempt with a batter other than the pitcher up, because if the runner is thrown out, the pitcher will be leading off the next inning. On a steal of second, a left-handed batter presents more of an obstacle to the catcher than a right-hander.

Certain pitches are better to steal on than others. For example, a count of nothing and two is a bad time to steal because the catcher is completely free to call for a pitchout. A count on which the batter is ahead is better—the catcher will be more reluctant to call for a pitchout in this situation, and the batter can afford to swing and miss the pitch to make the catcher's throw more difficult.

Certain types of pitches are also easier to steal on. If a knuckle ball is thrown, the catcher will have trouble just holding on to it, to say nothing of throwing it for the put-out. A breaking pitch is easier to steal on than a fastball because it takes more time to get to the catcher. And a pitch that is low and inside will require more time to throw to second than an outside pitch. Observing the pattern of pitches or, if possible, any giveaway movements of the pitcher before delivery may aid the runner in knowing what pitch will be thrown.

Double steal

The double steal is a play in which two bases are stolen simultaneously. It can involve runners on any combination of bases. The play is often attempted with runners on first and third. It is generally done with a weak man at bat and two outs, or with a strong batter with two strikes called against him. With less than two outs, the runner on third has other chances to score that should not be endangered with this risky play.

The runner on first initiates the play, starting with the pitch, and the runner on third takes a couple of steps down the base line and remains stationary, hoping to deceive the catcher as to the extent of his lead. When the catcher throws to second, the man on third goes home and the man going for second, if unable to make the base safely, allows himself to be caught in a rundown. Meanwhile the runner going home can score. A variation of this play is for the man on first to allow himself to be caught off base, whether stealing on the catcher in a delayed steal or stealing on the pitcher as he puts his foot on the rubber. Here the runner on third also breaks for the plate as soon as the defense tries to make the play on the man off first.

The runner on third must never allow himself to be bluffed. He runs for home only after the catcher (or pitcher) has thrown the ball. To counter this play, the man covering second will cut into the diamond for the throw and then make the play at the plate.

Double steal with men on first and second

If the man on second may be able to steal third, the man on first should take advantage of his teammate's speed. As the runner on second breaks for third, the runner on first moves toward second. Most often the throw will go to third and the runner going to second will be conceded the base. But an alert catcher may play to second, in which case the runner from first is on his own.

Rundowns

Runners attempting to steal are the most likely to get caught in rundowns. Since the defense will probably be trying to force the runner to commit himself and will run full speed for an easy and quick put-out, it's up to the runner to do everything possible to frustrate this strategy. He must put as much distance as he can between himself and the man with the ball. The object is to stay alive long enough to allow other runners to advance and to force as many throws as possible, hoping for an error.

If two players end up on the same base, the original occupant of the base is awarded it; however, the players should stay on base and wait for the decision of the umpire.

Ground balls

A runner on first advances on all ground balls. He must run hard and be prepared to slide to break up the double play.

With no one on first, a runner on second goes on any grounder except a hard hit ball to the third base side. On other balls hit to the left side, the runner has to use his judgment. Generally, on a ball hit to the left side of the shortstop, the runner should be able to make third. On a ball hit to the shortstop's right, the runner must wait to see if it goes through the infield. If it doesn't and he runs anyway, he'll either be thrown out at third or caught in a rundown. On balls hit to the right side of the infield, the runner should have no trouble making it to third if he has taken his proper lead. Any runner on second is in scoring position, so there's little point in his taking unnecessary risks to gain third base with two outs. However, with only one out, it is better for him to be on third, where a sacrifice can score him. The same fundamentals apply to a man on third; there's less reason to try to score with none out than there is with one.

With runners on second and third, none or one out, and the infield playing in, the runner on second has to know what the runner on third is going to do. He checks the coach for instructions. Usually, the runners won't advance with none out (unless, of course, the ball goes through the infield). With one out, the runner on third may go home on any grounder, expecially if the next hitter is weak. The offense is gambling that even on a ball hit directly to the drawn-in infielders, they may be nervous and hurry their throws somewhat.

A runner on third with first occupied and less than two outs must break for home on any ground ball in order to draw the play to home and avoid a double play. If the double play is made, it will be at the expense of a run. With none out and the infield back, a man on third advances on any standard ground ball.

Naturally, with two out and the count three and two, all runners go with the pitch.

Short fly balls

With less than two outs, the runner goes to a point from which he can return safely to base if the ball is caught. A runner on third tags up, especially if the infielder is forced to run toward the outfield for the catch. With less than two out and men on first and third, both men tag on a pop fly hit in back of first base: on a throw to home, the runner on first will make second easily; on a throw to second, the runner on third will score.

Long fly balls

Runners on second and third tag up. If the runner on first is fast, he may also tag up with one out, although he must be sure to make second safely. If he's thrown out, any run crossing the plate after the tag is nullified.

To tag up the runner watches the flight of the ball, resting his foot on the inside of the bag. His body should be slightly crouched, his feet pointing toward the next base. When the ball touches the fielder, the runner's weight must be on his front foot in order to make the first step with the back foot. Even if a runner feels he can't make the next base, he should fake a break in the hope of drawing a bad throw.

Chuck Tanner and Jim Enright

Born on July 4, 1929, Chuck Tanner learned more geography looking out the window of a minor league bus than he did in school in New Castle, Pennsylvania. His early travels as a minor league ballplayer took him to Owensboro, Kentucky; Eau Claire, Wisconsin; and Pawtucket, Rhode Island, before he graduated to the higher minors. Finally, nine years after he entered organized baseball, Tanner won promotion to the majors, where he spent six years. As a major leaguer, he won't be remembered as saving the best for last. In his first appearance at the plate, against Cincinnati in Milwaukee's County Stadium on April 12, 1955, Tanner rocked the first pitch for a pinch-hit home run. It was more or less downhill from there. In a 396-game career, he managed only 21 homers and a respectable, but not eye-catching .261 batting average. He's been telling his ballplayers, "Do as I say, not as I do," ever since.

As a manager, Tanner climbed the ladder much as he had as a ballplayer. In eight years he moved from Class A in the minors to Class AAA. When he led the Hawaii Islanders, the California Angels' Pacific Coast League affiliate, to a first-place finish in 1970, the White Sox finally noticed. They hired Tanner, their ninth manager since 1946, at the end of the 1970 season. A year later, Rollie Hemond, a fellow alumnus of the Angels' farm system, joined the Sox as personnel director. It was Hemond who acquired the players that Tanner would mold into a pennant-contending team.

It took Tanner less than two years to resurrect the White Sox. From their last-place finish in 1970, Tanner took the Sox to third place in 1971 and second place in 1972. The team that had been a 106-game loser in 1970 had become an 87-game winner in 1972. Suddenly, Chuck Tanner was manager of the year, and enthusiastic supporters were calling him a magician for transforming Dick Allen from a brooding recluse into a team leader.

Like most managers, Tanner is more at home speaking of baseball fundamentals than of the spiritual transformation of ballplayers. He demands that his players be as aggressive on defense as they are at the plate and on the bases. With the White Sox in eclipse in 1973 after a promising start, Tanner reiterates his credo. Winning, he says, is not good luck; it's playing the game properly.

A sportswriter for *Chicago Today*, Jim Enright has been around Chicago long enough to witness the rise and fall of a host of White Sox teams. Born in Sodus, Michigan, Enright has been writing sports since 1928. In 1937, he joined the *Chicago Evening American*, which became *Chicago Today*.